D1830085

Good News, Day by Day

Good News, Day by Day

Bible Reflections for Teens

by
Dee Bernhardt
Larry Schatz, FSC
Laurie Ziliak

Saint Mary's Press
Christian Brothers Publications
Winona, Minnesota

Genuine recycled paper with 10% post-consumer waste.
Printed with soy-based ink.

The publishing team included Carl Koch, development editor; Laurie A. Berg, copy editor; James H. Gurley, production editor; Hollace Storkel, typesetter; Cindi Ramm, cover designer; prepress, printing, and binding by the graphics division of Saint Mary's Press.

Printed in the United States of America

Printing: 9 8 7 6 5 4 3 2 1

Year: 2007 06 05 04 03 02 01 00 99

ISBN 0-88489-601-3

PREFACE

Welcome to *Good News, Day by Day.* We are pleased to share our reflections with you.

Each day's entry contains a Bible verse, a brief reflection, and a short prayer. For more about the Scripture passage, suggestions for further reading in your Bible are also included.

To get the most from the reflections, use them daily. Prayer can happen at any time of the day, but it's best to pick a specific time when you have at least five minutes of quiet time to think about what you are reading.

Read the Bible verse aloud several times—if you can—so that you hear the message in the words. Then read the reflection ideas and consider the question(s) at the end. You may want to start a prayer journal and write your responses to the questions in it. After you have given a question some thought, imagine God sitting right there with you, and address the short prayer directly to God. You may want to add your own thoughts or spend some time in silence with God as well.

You can check out the suggestions for further reading in your Bible immediately or at a later point in the day. These are to help you become more familiar with the Hebrew Scriptures and the Christian Testament of the Bible. We encourage you to consider using *The Catholic Youth Bible,* also published by Saint Mary's Press. *The Catholic Youth Bible* contains hundreds of study, prayer, and life application articles, many of which are connected to Bible passages used in *Good News, Day by Day.*

As you journey, consider that many others are joining with you in your devotions, using these same reflections, and enjoy the adventure of learning and praying the *Good News, Day by Day!*

MARY, MOTHER OF GOD

When the fullness of time had come, God sent his Son, born of a woman, born under the law, in order to redeem those who were under the law, so that we might receive adoption as children. (Galatians 4:4–5)

Today we celebrate the beginning of a new year and focus on the mother of Jesus, Mary, the human being who said yes to God and helped to change the world. Let us resolve to be like Mary, to say a heartfelt yes to bringing Jesus into our world every day of this year.

Dear God, as this year begins, help me to follow in Mary's footsteps each day. Let me resolve to be all that you have called me to be, and help me to live as your child each day.

January 2

When he was at table with them, he took the bread, blessed and broke it, and gave it to them. Then their eyes were opened, and they recognized him. (Luke 24:30–31)

After Jesus had risen, he walked along with some of his followers toward the town of Emmaus. His followers didn't immediately recognize him, even though he talked with them for quite a while. It was only when he broke the bread that they realized they were with Jesus. How many times do we see Jesus in the people we walk with? Do we see Jesus a little more when we stop and take time to eat with other people? When we spend time with others and get to know them, we are able to see Jesus in profound ways. In whom will you see Jesus today?

God, help me to see you in everyone I walk with today.

For more: Read the whole story of the journey to Emmaus (Luke 24:13–53).

I have called you by name, you are mine. (Isaiah 43:1)

We have heard many times in many ways: we have been called, we have been chosen, we are special to God. And yet it is easy to forget this. We have a special bond with God and God with us, in much the same way as we have a special bond with our family. No matter what happens, that bond will always be there, for God loves us. When we are angry with God or when we forget that God is with us, that bond of love will still be present and cannot be broken.

Loving God, thank you for loving me as part of your family. Help me to always be aware of your love for me.

For more: Read First Corinthians, chapter 13, and ask yourself how God has shown you the love that is talked about in this chapter.

ELIZABETH ANN SETON (1774–1821)

She opens her hand to the poor, and reaches out her hands to the needy. (Proverbs 31:20)

Elizabeth Ann Seton is the first person to be declared a saint who was born in the United States. She opened the first Catholic school in the United States and founded the Sisters of Charity. Clearly she is a woman who saw a need and moved ahead to meet that need. She once said, "The charity of our blessed Lord . . . was gentle, benevolent, and universal." Her legacy of Catholic schools and the Sisters of Charity is with us today.

O God, let my first goal today be to do your will; secondly, to do it in the way that you will it; and thirdly, to do it because it is your will. (Based on a prayer by Elizabeth Seton)

For God did not give us a spirit of cowardice, but rather a spirit of power and of love and of self-discipline. (2 Timothy 1:7)

God has given us a spirit of power and love. We have the power to love, and love changes everything. We have the power to love the genius in our history class, the power to love the person who does things we ourselves would never do, the power to love ourselves enough to abstain from unhealthy behaviors. Love is a powerful force—ask people who have felt that they were not loved at some point in their life. We have the spirit and power of love. Would others know that from looking at our life?

Gracious God, thank you for giving me the power to love and the spirit to love those who seem unlovable, even myself at times. Help me always to show your spirit of love and the power of that love to my friends and even to strangers.

For more: Read the story of Jesus and the woman who was caught in adultery (John 7:52—8:11).

EPIPHANY

In the time of King Herod, after Jesus was born in Bethlehem of Judea, wise men from the East came to Jerusalem, asking, "Where is the child who has been born king of the Jews? For we observed his star at its rising, and have come to pay him homage." (Matthew 2:1–2)

Today we celebrate the faith and the insight of the strange visitors who came to visit the baby Jesus. They saw a star, listened to God, and followed. After a difficult journey, they were eventually led to Jesus. In many ways we too are like the kings. God puts a star on our horizon that leads us on a difficult journey. Being Christian in this culture, especially as young people, is not easy. And yet if we follow the star of our faith, like the kings we will find Jesus, and we will truly be able to pay Jesus homage by the way we live our life.

God of the journey, help me always to follow your star, even when the way is long and difficult.

For more: Read about the wise men in Matthew, chapter 2. You probably know it, but have you read it lately?

You shall not murder. (Exodus 20:13)

This command seems pretty straightforward and easy, right? Not always—not if we see a person as more than just a body. A person is body *and* spirit. Therefore this command also means that we may not murder someone's spirit by talking behind their back or belittling their talent or making fun of them. Rather, we are called to support one another.

Gracious God, help me always to see the good in others, even in those I don't want to like, and always to work to build up their spirit, not to tear it down.

For more: Read Matthew 5:21–26, where Jesus talks about this commandment. Also read all the commandments found in Exodus, chapter 20.

January 8

In those days John the Baptist appeared in the wilderness of Judea, proclaiming, "Repent, for the kingdom of heaven has come near." (Matthew 3:1–2)

According to the image we are given of John the Baptist in the Bible, he was quite a character. He gave up everything, even his life, to spread the word, urging people to change their ways and to prepare themselves for the presence of God among them. Even though he was eccentric, we are called to be like John, for we are called to be witnesses to the presence of God among us by what we say and do. Are you being a good witness?

God, show me the way to be your witness to the world, and give me the courage to be an instrument of your presence.

For more: Read the story of Peter and his witness to Jesus in John 18:25–27 and John 21:15–19. Because Peter is human, it's a two-part story!

Then Jesus was led up by the Spirit into the wilderness to be tempted by the devil. (Matthew 4:1)

At times reading and studying about Jesus can be depressing. After all, he is divine and sinless. Are we supposed to be like that? Passages such as the preceding one remind us that Jesus was fully human, like us. He was not immune to temptation. Jesus was holy not because he was never exposed to sin but because he turned away from sin. We may not always make the right choice, but with God's grace we can choose rightly.

Loving God, help me to make choices that reflect your desire and love. Please lead me away from temptation, but when I find myself there, deliver me from evil.

For more: Read stories from one of the Gospels—Matthew, Mark, Luke, or John—and see how they portray Jesus. What aspects can you most identify with?

January 10

You are the light of the world. . . . Let your light shine before others, so that they may see your good works and give glory to your [God] in heaven. (Matthew 5:14–16)

Even a small light in a dark room is extremely powerful, for the room is no longer dark. This is why Jesus uses the image of light: even a little bit can change everything. We are asked to be a light of goodness and hope. Our light can and does make a difference. The light we shine by refusing to make fun of a person that everyone else picks on, changes the entire room for that person. How else can you be a light for others?

God of light, thank you for giving your light and life to me. May my light shine so that others may see it, and may others see you through me and come to know you better.

For more: Read John 8:12–20, in which Jesus asks no less of himself. Jesus says he is the light of the world.

Commit your way to Yahweh; trust in God who will act. (Psalm 37:5)

The funny thing about trust is that to learn to trust, we must trust! Spend some time today considering the ways you do and do not trust God. Ask yourself, Can I commit my way to a God whom I do not trust?

You know, God, trusting can be very hard for me sometimes. I want your will, my way. Please teach me to give more of the control in my life to you.

For more: Read Psalm 37, which speaks about trust and the patience we need when other people do not treat us fairly.

January 12

You shall not cheat one another, but you shall fear your God; for I am the Lord your God. (Leviticus 25:17)

Early in life we may do what is good out of fear. As we mature we may learn to do good out of love. Can you think of one area of your life as a child in which you were honest out of fear, but now you are honest out of love? in which you acted responsibly out of fear, but now out of love?

Dear God, sometimes I am afraid of you, but mostly I just forget you are there at all! Please help me to be more honest in my daily interactions so that I can grow away from my fear of punishment toward love of you.

For more: Look in John 8:31–32, to see why Jesus told those who believed in him that "the truth will make you free."

Now John wore clothing of camel's hair with a leather belt around his waist, and his food was locusts and wild honey. (Matthew 3:4)

Jesus and John the Baptist were cousins born only three months apart. Although John was an important messenger of God, he certainly did not conform to the dress or diet of his day. Can you think of anyone you know whom you ignore because of his or her strange appearance? Just because someone is different, does that mean that God does not live in them?

Dear God, keep me from judging others based on appearance. Remind me every day that who I am and who my friends are on the inside is much more important than what we wear on the outside.

For more: Check out Luke 12:22–34 to see what Jesus tells us is more important than food and clothing.

January 14

So now, O Israel, what does the Lord your God require of you? Only . . . to walk in all his ways, to love him, to serve the Lord your God with all your heart and with all your soul. (Deuteronomy 10:12)

That's all God wants, is it? That's a lot! It seems like the older we get, the more we are challenged to live our life according to God's values. Do you take your values as a Christian seriously?

Dear God, I'm not always sure that I can measure up to those around me. I turn to you for guidance, but your way seems out of reach. Help me to trust that you are there, supporting me in my search for the right values.

For more: Figuring out how to walk with, serve, and love God can be complicated. Look at Matthew 25:31–45 to find some practical help.

MARTIN LUTHER KING JR.

And remember, I am with you always, to the end of the age. (Matthew 28:20)

Martin Luther King Jr. spoke out and ultimately gave his life for the civil rights of all people. Few people have not heard his famous "I Have a Dream" speech. But Reverend King also had doubts, and this was one Scripture verse from which he took great strength. Where do you turn when you have doubts?

Always-present God, like Dr. King I sometimes have doubts. Help me to believe like him that someday, even though I'm a sinner, I'll hear your voice say to me, "I take you in and I bless you because you tried."

For more: Psalm 139 reminds us that God knows everything about us, even when we were in our mother's womb. Read over Psalm 139 and consider what your call to serve might be.

January 16

Beloved, do not imitate what is evil but imitate what is good. (3 John 1:11)

Does it sometimes seem that people who break the rules have the best lives? Their lives are certainly exciting, yet when we speak with them on a deeper level, we often find a loneliness that is hard to explain. Try to think of someone you know whose life reflects the deep happiness that only goodness can bring.

Dear God, I am so tempted to imitate what I know is evil, just because it looks like fun! Please give me the wisdom to recognize the long-term consequences of my actions. Thank you for the people I know who through their life teach me what is good.

For more: The Third Letter of John is a very short letter. Try reading it aloud slowly. Are you more like Diotrephes or Demetrius?

Do not be a hypocrite before others, and keep watch over your lips. (Sirach 1:29)

It is easy for us to talk about other people. Conversations that start out as sharing the news can easily become gossip sessions. As Christians we are called to be kind and merciful. Today when you talk about another person, make sure that what you say is kind.

God of compassion, when I get together with my friends, I find it easy to judge those who are not like me and to trash their reputation. Help me so I talk about other people just as I would want them to talk about me.

For more: The Apostle Paul lists clear instructions on how to live as a young Christian in the First Letter to Timothy. It's worth reading.

January 18

Let no one despise your youth, but set the believers an example in speech and conduct, in love, in faith, in purity. (1 Timothy 4:12)

No matter how old we are, some people always see us as "kids." The older we get, the more frustrating this can be. But at other times, we claim that we're not old enough to know better, when in our heart we truly do know that we haven't set a good example. Perhaps today is a good day to examine your actions to see what kind of an example you are.

Dear God, inspire me to set a good example no matter what my age. I am young, but I can, with your power, love other people.

For more: Read Proverbs, chapter 2, to find good advice on how to become wise.

Noah did this; he did all that God commanded him. (Genesis 6:22)

When we think of Noah and the ark, we think of how faithful and smart Noah was to follow God the way that he did. Yet imagine how unpopular he must have been, building that big boat in his yard when it wasn't even raining. Consider what you would do if God asked you to do something so publicly unpopular. But doesn't being a Christian sometimes call us to unpopular behavior?

Saving God, even knowing that Jesus died for me, I sometimes lose sight of my responsibility to follow through with my faith. When I falter, please remind me of Noah and his family, who endured public ridicule because of their strong and sure faith.

For more: Check out the three young people in Daniel, chapter 3, who chose to go through a fiery furnace rather than deny their faith.

January 20

Rejoice always, pray without ceasing, give thanks in all circumstances; for this is the will of God in Christ Jesus for you. (1 Thessalonians 5:16–18)

Sometimes we meet people who always seem to be happy, and we might be tempted to believe that these people have lives free from bad experiences. Some suffering is part of every life, so it may help to remember that we can, with God's help, decide to be joyful even in the face of disaster. Decide to focus on the good today, and see how your day shapes up.

Dear God, when life is not going my way, I want other people to make it right again. I sometimes choose to shower my unhappiness on whomever I meet. Help me to concentrate on your blessings this day so that I can be an inspiration to others and reflect my faith in you.

For more: The First Letter to the Thessalonians, chapter 5, advises us on how to live so that we are prepared for the second coming of Christ. Try to live a different verse of this chapter each day for a week.

God is not a human being, that he should lie, or a mortal, that he should change his mind. (Numbers 23:19)

Some of us are blessed enough to have someone that we can trust with any secret in the world. Imagine how trustworthy God must be if human confidences can be that strong! Take some time today to trust God with one of the secrets from the silence of your heart.

Patient God, move in my heart and shine your light on the dark corners so that I can give over my secrets to you. Please strengthen my trust that you are worthy of my highest confidence.

For more: In Numbers, chapter 23, we hear the story of Balaam and his prophecies. Take some time to consider if you would have been as trusting of God as Balaam was.

January 22

At Gibeon the Lord appeared to Solomon in a dream by night; and God said, "Ask what I should give you." (1 Kings 3:5)

We do not often hear of God making such an extravagant offer as this one! When Solomon answers, he asks to know what is best for his kingdom. If God made this offer to you, what would you ask for?

God of all goodness, my first thought upon hearing this question has a lot to do with my own gain. Help me to remember that I am only one small part of a much larger Kingdom, in which you reign.

Get the whole story of Solomon by reading the First Book of Kings in your Bible, starting with 1 Kings, chapter 2, in which Solomon's father gives him some truly inspirational advice.

Shun youthful passions and pursue righteousness, faith, love, and peace, along with those who call on the Lord from a pure heart. (2 Timothy 2:22)

Passion can be a dangerous word because we often associate passion with physical love and lust, but to be great at anything, even at living like Christ, requires passion. Passionate people become totally absorbed in and committed to the object of their passion. Can you let go of or shun the passions that distract you from following God? How can you be passionate about Christ?

Dear God, give me passion for truth, for service of my neighbor, and for hope in the future. Please strengthen my resolve to pursue your way and to become passionate for those things that will endure.

For more: The Song of Solomon speaks freely and openly about the virtues of passion. Read this beautiful love poem in your Bible today.

FRANCIS DE SALES

I give you a new commandment, that you love one another. Just as I have loved you, you also should love one another. (John 13:34)

Francis de Sales lived during a difficult time for the church. He preached love and moderation when the church was splitting apart. He took his time praying and thinking about decisions before taking any action on them. His bottom line on every decision was love. In one of his writings, Francis reminds us, "A single Our Father said with feeling has greater value than many said quickly and hurriedly."

Say the Lord's Prayer (the Our Father) slowly and thoughtfully.

For more: When Jesus' Apostles asked him to teach them how to pray, he taught them the Lord's Prayer. You can find the story of this special prayer in Luke, chapter 11.

So be careful not to forget the covenant that the Lord your God made with you, and not to make for yourselves an idol in the form of anything that the Lord your God has forbidden you. (Deuteronomy 4:23)

We are easily tricked into worshiping idols: the idols of success, wealth, fame, even youth. These may not look like idols, but when they become more important to us than our faith and trust in God, that's what they are. Do you have any idols in your life?

God of mercy, of course I want to stay on your good side, but I want to be comfortable too. Please help me to remember that all my successes are good as long as I keep my priorities straight, with you at the top of the list.

For more: Read Mark 10:17–31, the story of a man who put the idol of his possessions ahead of following Jesus.

January 26

I treasure your [word] within my heart, that I may not sin against you. (Psalm 119:11)

Whenever our friends give us compliments, or family members let us know that they love us, their words stay alive in our heart and are easily remembered. This psalm reminds us that the word of God belongs in that same special corner of our heart and mind. With God's word in our heart, our actions can be guided by it. Take some time today to consider which stories or quotes from the word of God have a place in your heart.

Dear God, when I remember the respect of my friends and the love of my family, it really helps me to live what I believe. Help me to treasure your word so that I will be able to take strength in it each day of my life.

For more: Read Luke 4:14–30 to learn how powerful the word of God was in Jesus' life.

Jesus said to them, "Truly I tell you, the tax collectors and the prostitutes are going into the kingdom of God ahead of you." (Matthew 21:31)

This verse marks the end of a parable about two sons. One does what he was asked to do; the other says that he will but never gets to it. The point is that actions speak louder than words. Today consider the differences between some of your good intentions and your actions.

Wise God, help my actions match my good intentions. Please open my ears so that I can hear and do what you say, what you want.

For more: Sometimes we can get sidetracked. Read John 8:1–11 to see how Jesus dealt with one woman who had lost her way.

January 28

Do not abandon old friends, for new ones cannot equal them. A new friend is like new wine; when it has aged, you can drink it with pleasure. (Sirach 9:10)

Friends can be complicated. We must leave some behind because they are leading us into trouble, but there are those who stand by us through all the trials of our life. Today think of an old friend, and write him or her a letter or an e-mail, even if you cannot send it.

Dear God, thank you for the gift of friendship that makes life bearable many times. Help me to cherish my true friends, and give me the wisdom to leave the false ones behind.

For more: Read John 15:12–17 to find out who Jesus' friends are.

Peter said to him, "Though all become deserters because of you, I will never desert you." (Matthew 26:33)

Peter, always the most vocal of the Apostles, just had to prove to Jesus that he was the number-one Apostle, so he made a bold promise instead of listening to what Jesus was telling him. We too sometimes promise things that we really cannot control. Today try listening carefully to others and learning from them instead of making bold promises.

Dear God, the trouble with me is that I truly believe I can follow through on my bold promises. Please help me to consider the cost of my words before they get out of my mouth.

For more: Matthew 26:69–75 tells us the ending to this story. What would you have done?

January 30

MOHANDAS GANDHI

But Jesus said to him, "Do not stop him; for whoever is not against you is for you." (Luke 9:50)

Gandhi, a Hindu, spent much of his life studying Christianity. His life of passive resistance in India poses a real challenge to Christians because we are called to that way of living. Nonviolent resistance was the loving means that led to India's freedom from British rule. Gandhi remarked, "The means may be likened to a seed, the end to a tree; and there is just the same inviolable connection between the means and the end as there is between the seed and the tree." Today consider the Gospel challenge to live your life guided only by love.

Dear God, it is easy for me to write off those of different faiths than my own because they are not Christian. Please help me to realize that the most important path for me to monitor is my own.

For more: In Luke 9:46–48 we learn who is the greatest in the eyes of Jesus.

JOHN BOSCO

Let the little children come to me; do not stop them; for it is to such as these that the kingdom of God belongs. (Mark 10:14)

John Bosco had a difficult childhood while growing up in Italy. So when he became a priest, he opened homes and schools for homeless teens. He loved these street kids, but needed patience with them. He would remind himself that Jesus "treated sinners with a kindness and affection that caused some to be shocked, . . . others to gain hope in God's mercy." Can you think of any cause to which you would dedicate your whole life?

Dear God, John Bosco gave his whole life to the service of the church and the education of homeless young people. Please show me where I belong, so that my life will also make a positive difference.

For more: Read Mark 10:13–16 to hear how Jesus dealt with the little children.

February 1

The Lord bless you and keep you. (Numbers 6:24)

These days the only time we hear people say, "God bless you," seems to be when we sneeze or when we visit our elderly relatives. Yet the Bible reminds us that we must bless one another and also bless God. Give a blessing to a friend or a family member today. The blessing may take the form of praise or thanks too.

Merciful God, I praise and bless you because you have given me so much to be grateful for. Sometimes blessing someone else feels awkward. Give me the right words to share a blessing. You have given me wonderful blessings, so help me share them with those around me.

For more: When Mary's cousin Elizabeth saw her pregnant with Jesus, she gave Mary a blessing. Read Luke 1:39–45.

PRESENTATION OF THE LORD

When the time came for their purification according to the law of Moses, they brought [Jesus] up to Jerusalem, to present him to the Lord. (Luke 2:22)

According to the Law of Moses, parents had to present their firstborn son to God, so they did. As devout Jews, Jesus' parents followed the Law. They had to travel a long way and wait their turn, but they did it because it was the right thing to do. Would you take all that trouble to maintain a tradition that affirms your relationship with God?

Holy One, when it comes to laws that benefit me directly, I'm all for respecting the law and waiting my turn. I'm afraid that I fall short of your parents when it comes to your laws. Give me the patience to trust and follow in your ways.

For more: Find out which law Jesus felt was the most important by reading Matthew 22:34–40.

February 3

So if you have been raised with Christ, seek the things that are above, where Christ is, seated at the right hand of God. (Colossians 3:1)

Seeking the ways of Christ can be difficult if we don't really know where to begin looking. At baptism we are raised with Christ; now we encounter Christ through meditating on the Bible, listening to wise and good people, and praying. Have you made a commitment with your life to follow Christ?

Dear God, on this day I renew the commitment made at baptism. I commit my life to following you. Please give me lots of road signs so I stay on the right path.

For more: Read Psalm 119:1–20 and consider how you can seek God with your whole heart.

The Lord is not slow about his promise, as some think of slowness, but is patient with you, not wanting any to perish, but all to come to repentance. (2 Peter 3:9)

In our culture we get into the habit of thinking, Three strikes and you're out! Peter reminds us that God doesn't think that way. Thank God today for being patient with you.

Forgiving God, you are truly loving to put up with me sometimes. It's a wonder that you don't just call it quits with the human race, and with me in particular. Thank you for your patience. You promised that you would never give up on me. Help me to not give up on you.

For more: Read Second Peter, chapter 3, to see Peter's response to the impatient people of his day.

February 5

Seek advice from any wise person and do not despise any useful counsel. (Tobit 4:18)

Sometimes we meet a wise person and we know it. Other times it takes longer for the wisdom to sink in. We do not always want to hear what a wise person has to say. Today consider who the wise people are in your life. You might start a journal in which you write down little bits of wisdom that you hear from people or have read.

Dear God, help me to recognize the wisdom that I encounter each day so that I can become more wise and more grounded in you. Thank you for the people you have sent into my life to point me in the right direction.

For more: Spend some time with Psalm 77 and write your thoughts in your journal.

In the morning, while it was still very dark, [Jesus] got up and went out to a deserted place, and there he prayed. (Mark 1:35)

God wants to hear from us. All we have to do is take a little time and start a conversation. The trouble is that we get distracted. Jesus got up early and isolated himself so that he could pray. Today take at least one minute and pray in your own words. You have at least a spare minute.

Dear God, I know the prayers I learned at church, but they don't always express what I'm trying to say. Please teach me to start my day off in conversation with you.

For more: Look in Jeremiah, chapter 1, to find the story of a young person's conversation with God.

February 7

Let each of you look not to your own interests, but to the interests of others. Let the same mind be in you that was in Christ Jesus. (Philippians 2:4–5)

Most of us excel at watching out for ourselves. Jesus' compassion stood out as unusual among the people of his day because he reached out to all the people that everyone else rejected. Take some time today to reach out to someone outside your usual group of friends.

Dear God, I am comfortable in my group of friends, and I'm not sure I want to reach beyond my boundaries to welcome others. Please show me how to be more compassionate toward others, and lead me to the friends I need to support me in following you.

For more: Read John, chapter 8, for an example of Jesus' great compassion. With whom do you identify?

But Joseph said to them, "Do not be afraid! Am I in the place of God?" (Genesis 50:19)

Joseph went through a lot in his life. He suffered greatly at the hands of his brothers, and was even sold by them. Yet in the end, he not only forgave them but he welcomed them back into his new life. Is there someone in your family that you need to forgive?

God of mercy, people like Joseph seem so unreal. Help me to remember that your Spirit can guide me to forgiveness in my heart and to open myself to the grace of that guidance.

For more: The whole story of Joseph challenges us to reconsider how good we have it. Check it out in Genesis, chapter 37.

February 9

Cast all your anxiety on [God], because [God] cares for you. (1 Peter 5:7)

Have you ever been really worried about something that you were afraid to share with anyone, even your closest friends? That's what makes a relationship with Jesus so wonderful. He is always here to listen and care. Share something with him today from the secret places in your heart.

Dear God, I have been carrying this around for a long time. Now I'm inviting you to help me carry it. (Mention your secret concern.) Thank you for caring enough to help me out.

For more: Look in Matthew, chapter 7, where Jesus reminds us not to judge others, but instead to approach God for what we need.

The kingdom of heaven may be compared to a king who gave a wedding banquet for his son. (Matthew 22:2)

In many of the parables or stories that Jesus told, he described heaven in terms of a party. In this story from Matthew, we hear about someone who refused to wear the robe that was provided and so got kicked out. We are invited to the banquet of heaven. Are you willing to "put on" Christ so that you can stay?

Dear God, I want to share in your banquet, and I do try to reflect you in all that I do. Please be patient with me as I continue to grow into my understanding of what it means to follow you.

For more: Read the whole parable of the wedding feast in Matthew, chapter 22.

February 11

Desire without knowledge is not good, and one who moves too hurriedly misses the way. (Proverbs 19:2)

This proverb urges us to check out things before rushing into them. Slow down! It can be too easy to make a quick decision, only to regret it later. Spend some time today asking God to guide you in a decision that you are making.

God of patient listening, at times I wish I had more options, but at other times the choices seem to be too many. I am asking you today to walk with me and guide me through this decision I am making. (Tell God about the decision.)

For more: The Book of Proverbs is full of advice for us. Read chapter 19 to learn more about the virtue of integrity.

ABRAHAM LINCOLN

Above all, my beloved, do not swear, either by heaven or by earth or by any other oath, but let your "Yes" be yes and your "No" be no, so that you may not fall under condemnation. (James 5:12)

We know that Abraham Lincoln was a man who took a stand. The following is something Lincoln said that we should think about: "My concern is not whether God is on our side; my great concern is to be on God's side, for God is always right."

Dear God, I am working on taking a stand on many things: with my parents, the rest of my family, and my friends. Please help me to consider what I say before I say it, so that my word can stand strong, like Abraham Lincoln's.

For more: In Sirach (Ecclesiasticus), starting at chapter 51, verse 13, read the poem about how to seek wisdom and how to become a person of your word.

February 13

Do no evil, and evil will never overtake you. (Sirach 7:1)

Some books of the Bible surprise us with practical insights about everyday life. Sirach is one of those books. Sometimes we need to learn the obvious from someone else to really hear it. Today consider a time when you did something you shouldn't have done and it caught up with you.

Dear God, the trouble with me is that I don't always recognize evil as evil until after the fact, and by then it is too late! Please inspire me to walk in your light so that I will not need to struggle with evil at all.

For more: Read Sirach, chapter 7, to find other ways to become wise and to avoid evil.

SAINT VALENTINE'S DAY

We love because he first loved us. (1 John 4:19)

We celebrate loving and being loved on this special day. Of course most of us find it easier to love someone who loves us first, and that's what this verse is about. God loves us first and always; we only need to respond to that love. Imagine God sending you a valentine today. What would it say inside?

God who is love, on this day of celebrating love, I want to remind you that I love you. Even when I sometimes walk away or seem disinterested, please know that you have a special place in my heart.

For more: Loving God can appear to be an overwhelming task. Read First John, chapter 4, to hear some ways to start.

February 15

I have set my bow in the clouds, and it shall be a sign of the covenant between me and the earth. (Genesis 9:13)

A rainbow arching over a valley or a city skyline is a beautiful sight. The next time you see one, remind yourself of this passage in Genesis. Imagine it as a sign of God's eternal love for us.

O God, author of all that is good and beautiful, thank you for the gift of the rainbow and your covenant with us. Open our eyes to the signs of your love all around us.

For more: Spend time repeatedly praying Genesis 9:13.

Now therefore revere the Lord, and serve him in sincerity and in faithfulness. (Joshua 24:14)

The word *revere* is not one we use a lot, but it is the root of the word *reverence.* What does it mean to revere the Lord? How can you serve the Lord today "in sincerity and in faithfulness"?

O great and holy God, we your people revere you. Help us to witness to others our reverence for you, and let us always serve you faithfully and sincerely.

For more: Read Joshua 24:14–15 in a study Bible.

February 17

The Lord came and stood there, calling as before, "Samuel! Samuel!" And Samuel said, "Speak, for your servant is listening." (1 Samuel 3:10)

What a wonderful response to God: "Speak, for your servant is listening." Try to make that your prayer today. Quiet yourself, and then slowly repeat Samuel's simple prayer several times.

Speak, Lord, for your servant is listening.

For more on prayer, read all of First Samuel, chapter 3.

David and all the house of Israel were dancing before the Lord with all their might, with songs and lyres and harps and tambourines and castanets and cymbals. (2 Samuel 6:5)

We don't usually associate dancing with worshiping God, but for David and his people, they were clearly connected. Why do we often hesitate to consider dancing and singing as ways to worship God? Let loose. If you know a hymn, hum it or sing it.

Dear God, help me to overcome my somber attitudes about religion and worship. Help me to praise you with all my being. Let me not be afraid to sing and dance for you.

For more: Pray Psalm 98.

February 19

My child, keep my words and store up my commandments with you; keep my commandments and live, keep my teachings as the apple of your eye. (Proverbs 7:1–2)

Ask yourself: How well do I keep God's words with me? Do I strive to keep God's commandments? Do I treasure the teachings of God? Ask your Creator's views on your commandment-keeping.

Dear God, I ask your help in striving to keep your word. Let your words and your teachings truly become "the apple of my eye." Help me to live the good life.

For more: Read about God's two great commandments in Matthew 22:37–40.

[Jesus said,] "Love your enemies and pray for those who persecute you." (Matthew 5:44)

Let's be honest: we all know people we don't like, and we probably know people who don't like us. It's not enough to not be mean to them or to wish them no harm. We are to pray for them—pray for their health and happiness and pray in thanksgiving for their lives. Maybe Jesus has something here, for in praying for them, we may begin to see them differently.

God of love, I know that you love all your children and want us all to live together in peace and happiness. Show me how to pray for those who persecute me.

For more: Turn to Luke 23:34, and read of Jesus' final hours on the cross. Jesus follows his own advice.

February 21

So do not worry about tomorrow, for tomorrow will bring worries of its own. Today's trouble is enough for today. (Matthew 6:34)

Jesus obviously didn't live in the twentieth century. How can we not be anxious in these busy times? Nonetheless Jesus tells us not to worry. Jesus does not ask us not to think about tomorrow, but rather not to be anxious about it. It's easy to get so stressed out over a big test that we start getting stressed about everything else. Here is wisdom: pay attention to one day at a time. Prepare for the test but don't stress. Stay focused, and pray for strength, wisdom, and peace!

Gentle God, it's easy to become obsessed with the details of my life. Help me to keep them in focus and always to turn to you for guidance and strength.

For more: Read the story of Mary and Martha (Luke 10:38–42). How do you think each of these women would respond to Matthew 6:34?

GEORGE WASHINGTON

I will make of you a great nation, and I will bless you, and make your name great, so that you will be a blessing. (Genesis 12:2)

These words from Genesis are the words spoken by God to Abraham, a first ancestor of Judaism, Christianity, and Islam. George Washington is considered to be a founder of the United States. What would Washington say today were he to look upon the city that bears his name and the country he served as its first president? What makes a nation great? Is the United States a blessing?

Dear God, on this day we pause to thank you for the women and men who have heard your call to leadership and responded. We stand on their shoulders. Help us to continue to make our nation great, as you would have us great: that is, a nation of peace, justice, charity, and community.

February 23

[Jesus] . . . said to them: "Listen and understand: it is not what goes into the mouth that defiles a person, but it is what comes out of the mouth that defiles. . . . What comes out of the mouth proceeds from the heart, and this is what defiles." (Matthew 15:10–11,18)

Gossip kills. It kills the spirit and self-esteem of the person who is at the center of the gossip, and it can kill possible future friendships for that person. More important, gossip kills the people who are doing the gossiping, for every time we gossip, we kill a little kernel of goodness in our heart and take in a little piece of destructive evil. Are you becoming a gossip?

Bless the words of my mouth, O God, that I may resist the desire to tear others down. Help me keep my heart pure and my words supportive, encouraging, and hopeful.

For more: Gossip is a form of judgment. See what Jesus says about it in Matthew 7:1–5, Mark 4:24–25, or Luke 6:37–42.

A Canaanite woman from that region came out and started shouting, "Have mercy on me, Lord, Son of David." . . . He answered, "I was sent only to the lost sheep of the house of Israel." But she came and knelt before him, saying, "Lord, help me." (Matthew 15:22–25)

For this quote to make sense, you really need to know the whole story. Jews and Canaanites rejected one another. When the woman asks Jesus for help, he responds that he did not come to help non-Jews. She argues that he should help everyone. Jesus eventually changes his thinking and helps her. Challenging a person to grow like this is okay, as long as it's done in a caring manner. Here the woman challenges Jesus. His response told the world that Jesus would save non-Jews too.

Merciful God, sometimes it's hard to confront people about difficult issues. Give me the words to help others grow, not to tear them down. Give me the courage to actually challenge others when it is good to do so.

For more: Read the whole story in Matthew 15:21–28.

February 25

Teach me your way, Yahweh, and I will obey you faithfully; give me an undivided heart. (Psalm 86:11)

What does it mean to serve God with an undivided heart? What does it mean to divide our heart? What keeps us from loving and serving God wholeheartedly?

Pray this verse several times slowly, and repeat it through the day: Teach me your way; give me an undivided heart.

For more: Read all of Psalm 86.

Rejoice, young man [and woman], while you are young, and let your heart cheer you in the days of your youth. (Ecclesiastes 11:9)

Many people—maybe most people—dread growing old. They envy youth and strive to look younger. Take some time today to simply enjoy being young and full of energy. Don't let all the pressures facing you get you down. Rejoice! But remember, getting older has its gifts too.

God, life is your gift. Help me to appreciate my own youth and all the energy I have. Let me make the most of my youth in order to give you glory. Let me have a cheerful heart through the tough days too.

For more: See Ecclesiastes 11:7–10.

February 27

Come to me, all you that are weary and are carrying heavy burdens, and I will give you rest. (Matthew 11:28)

February can be a long, dreary month when snow has blanketed the ground for months. How do we cope with the February blahs? Have you ever unloaded on God? God is the best listener around. Our faith and our God are sources of hope, especially when we are feeling hopeless, but we need to go to God.

Gentle God, thank you for being with me in my struggles and for carrying my burdens. May I always be open to your hope. I come to you for rest and for hope.

For more: Even Jesus unloaded on God; check out Matthew 26:36–46, Mark 14:32–42, or Luke 22:39–46.

Let those who are friendly with you be many, but let your advisers be one in a thousand. (Sirach 6:6)

An adviser is a friend or a trusted adult that we can confide in and whose advice we can rely on. Who serves as an adviser in your life? If you cannot think of anyone, who is someone you could seek out for those times when you need counsel or advice?

God, thank you for my friends, and thank you especially for those individuals whom I can trust and in whom I can confide. Help me to be a good friend and not to offer advice unless I am asked to do so.

For more on friendship, see Sirach 6:5–17.

February 29

For where two or three are gathered in my name, I am there among them. (Matthew 18:20)

Do you ever get tired of people hassling you to go to church? Does God really care if we go? The answer is that we don't go to church for ourselves. Jesus tells us that he is with us in a special way when we gather together in his name. We experience God in a different way when we gather with our community to give praise and thanks. That can't be done at home. Ponder your involvement with a community of faith.

Jesus, thank you for your church, the community of believers that you have gathered. May I continue to be part of that community, growing and learning from it.

For more: Read about the early church and what it meant to Paul in Romans, chapter 16.

Jesus said, . . . "If you wish to be perfect, go, sell your possessions, and give the money to the poor, and you will have treasure in heaven; then come, follow me." (Matthew 19:21)

Jesus is pretty clear: being a nice person simply isn't enough. Though this command is tough and, some would argue, quite unrealistic, there are things we can do. Give clothes that you never wear to charity. Perhaps go without some treat for a week and give the money that you would have spent on it to your favorite charity. Get together with your friends and have a rummage sale for a good cause. Though we may not be ready to be missionaries just yet, we can still help poor people.

I am grateful for my many blessings, generous God, for I know that I am well cared for. May I always be mindful of those who go without and of my duty to care for them.

For more: Read the whole story in Matthew 19:16–22. Can you identify with the young man who questions Jesus?

March 2

You shall love your neighbor as yourself. (Matthew 22:39)

Do your friends treat you the way you want to be treated? Chances are they do, or they wouldn't be friends. How about those who are not your friends? Do they respect you the way that you want to be respected? Do you respect them the way you would want to be respected? When you are in a difficult situation, ask yourself, How would I want to be treated if the situation were reversed? Chances are you'll get some new insight into the situation.

God of all, give me the vision and integrity to always respect people and to treat them as I would want to be treated.

For more: Jesus takes it one step further; see Luke 7:36–50.

Truly I tell you, just as you did it to one of the least of these who are members of my family, you did it to me. (Matthew 25:40)

Christ dwells in each of us. Therefore Christ is in every person that we meet. It is up to us to find Christ in each person, as difficult as that can be at times. Christ is in our teachers, our friends, our parents, our neighbors—in every single person. Everything we do or say to another human being, we do or say to Christ. Are we doing and saying things worthy of Christ?

God, I know that you dwell in every person on earth, for you love each one of us. Help me to see your face in each person and to treat them as you.

For more: See John 14:15–26, especially verse 23. The Spirit does dwell in each of us.

March 4

[Jesus said,] "Whoever does the will of God is my brother and sister and mother." (Mark 3:35)

Jesus made it clear that we are all connected. All of us who do the will of God (or at least try to do the will of God) are members of the family of God, the Body of Christ, sharing a common faith. And yet being a member of a family is not without obligations, such as caring for one another, sharing our material goods when necessary, and praying for and with one another. How do you help care for this family to which you belong?

Gentle Parent of us all, thank you for making me part of your family and for connecting me to so many wonderful people. May I always be grateful for my family.

For more: See John 19:25–27.

All things can be done for the one who believes. (Mark 9:23)

This true story of one young woman has been repeated many times. She spent her first semester of college partying and drinking. By the end of the semester, she was on academic probation and struggling socially. One January night she attempted suicide. She survived, left school, went home, took a good, long look at her life, and got help. She returned to school and is now close to graduation. She learned to believe in herself, and that made all the difference. It's true, all things are possible for those who believe in God's grace.

I know that you believe in me, God, for you have called me by name. I pray that I may have the courage to believe in myself.

For more: Jesus believed in Peter; see John 21:15–19.

March 6

And [Jesus] entered the temple and began to drive out those who were selling and those who were buying in the temple, and he overturned the tables of the money changers. (Mark 11:15)

Is it okay to be angry? We seem to get conflicting messages: we should always love others, and yet even Jesus got angry. Love does not preclude anger. It's okay—even helpful—to be angry at times. The dilemma comes in how we deal with our anger. If we act out of our anger in a way that is intended to be hurtful, we're not doing anyone any favors, including ourselves. But acting out of our anger in a way that lovingly points to the truth, as Jesus did in the Temple, can be a holy gift.

I know that anger is natural, God. Help me to act out of my anger in a loving way, and forgive me for the times I have been hurtful because of my anger.

For more: Look at Mark 3:5. The incident in the Temple wasn't the only time Jesus got angry.

I heard the voice of the Lord saying, "Whom shall I send, and who will go for us?" And I said, "Here am I; send me!" (Isaiah 6:8)

God calls us mostly through human need: a crying child, a lonely grandparent, a starving homeless person, a friend who needs tutoring. How open are you to God's call in your life? If you sense that God is calling or sending you forth, how willing are you to respond as Isaiah did, "Here am I, Lord; send me"?

God, you are always available for us. Help us to realize that you are not so much interested in our ability or our inability, but rather in our availability. Here am I, God; send me!

For more: Read Isaiah 67:1–13.

INTERNATIONAL WOMEN'S DAY

A woman came to [Jesus] with an alabaster jar of very costly ointment, and she poured it on his head as he sat at the table. . . . [Jesus said,] "Truly I tell you, wherever this good news is proclaimed in the whole world, what she has done will be told in remembrance of her." (Matthew 26:6,13)

In Jesus' time, rulers were signified by anointing. This unnamed woman symbolically anointed Jesus as the Messiah, leading Jesus to recognize that her action was part of the Gospel proclamation. On International Women's Day, take time to remember all the women in your life who have done amazing things and are in danger of being forgotten.

Thank you, God, for the amazing women who have walked this earth, many of whom I do not know by name, and for the way they have made the world a better place.

For more: check out the Book of Ruth and the Book of Esther.

The world and all that is in it belong to Yahweh, the earth and all who live on it. (Psalm 24:1)

This is God's world. Like renters or visitors in a national park, we are here for only a short time. Like renters or visitors, even though we don't own the earth, we need to take care of it. How do you treat the earth: as God's? as your personal property to do with as you please?

O God, this world is yours. You have given us the opportunity to live in it, but only for a while. Let us never forget that all this earth and all of us belong to you.

March 10

I will pour out my spirit on all flesh; your sons and your daughters shall prophesy, your old men shall dream dreams, and your young men shall see visions. (Joel 2:28)

Do you have a vision that guides your life? What are your dreams? Do you seek God's help in determining God's vision for your life?

O God, you have planted deep within each of us a vision of who we are and what you are calling us to. Open me to the power of your dreams and your vision for my life.

A soft answer turns away wrath, but a harsh word stirs up anger. (Proverbs 15:1)

Such a simple proverb, but so much truth in it! How often do we make a tense situation worse by a cutting remark? Try a gentle response, the "soft answer," the next time you are in conflict.

Patient God, your Son, Jesus, showed us the way of gentleness. Give me the strength and determination to avoid harsh words and cutting remarks. Help me to master the soft answer.

March 12

As you have done, it shall be done to you; your deeds shall return on your own head. (Obadiah 1:15)

"What goes around comes around." This is a contemporary way of saying the same thing Obadiah said centuries ago. What if all that we did in our life, both bad and good, would come back to us?

O God, help me to plant seeds of goodness so that I may reap a harvest of good things in my life. Let me realize that everything I do has a ripple effect. Help me make good waves.

For more: See the Book of Obadiah.

SUSAN B. ANTHONY (1820–1906)

So God created humankind in [God's own] image, in the image of God [they were] created . . . ; male and female [God] created them. (Genesis 1:27)

Many of the rights that women today may take for granted, they have because of the courage and vision of Susan B. Anthony, an American pioneer of equality for women. She struggled to help women achieve the God-given dignity that is stated so powerfully in the first account of creation. She told people: "I look for the day when . . . the only criterion of excellence or position shall be the ability, honor, and character of the individual without regard to whether he or she be male or female. And this time will come."

God, we are created in your image, male and female. Help me to act for the rights of others and to see your image in the face of everyone I meet, especially those deprived of their dignity.

March 14

God saw everything that [had been] made, and indeed, it was very good. (Genesis 1:31)

Each of us at times wonders exactly how good we really are. Were we a mistake of God's? a first draft? Of course not! God sees everything, including us, and it is very good. Think about God looking upon your life today. What would please God? Are there some things you would change with God's help?

Dear God, thank you for making me the person I am. Although I do not appreciate some things about myself, I am happy to know that you find them, and me, very good.

For more: In the Book of Job, Job speaks directly to God about why he was ever born. Read Job, chapter 38, to hear God's response.

Give to everyone who begs from you, and do not refuse anyone who wants to borrow from you. (Matthew 5:42)

This message of the Gospel can seem impossible. Who can afford to give as much as this? Yet Jesus continually preached that we need to do a bit extra, giving more than just our castoffs. Can you stretch yourself enough to be unusually generous today?

Dear God, I want to be generous, but I know that some people take advantage of me. Then I feel used. Help me to remember that my giving pleases you and that what happens after I give is not in my hands.

For more: Matthew, chapter 5, contains many practical teachings for us today.

March 16

Who can detect failings? From hidden faults forgive me. (Psalm 19:12)

In Psalm 19 we hear a lot about the law of God and how important it is for us to follow it. But the psalmist ends with a few verses that ask God to help us figure out where we can go. Ask God to help you with your hidden faults.

Living God, some days I honestly believe that I am following your will and your way, not straying. On those days help me to remember that I am capable of misleading myself, so I must turn to you.

For more: Read Psalm 19 slowly, and underline any verse that stands out to you.

PATRICK

"Lord, if another member of the church sins against me, how often should I forgive? As many as seven times?" Jesus said to him, "Not seven times, but, I tell you, seventy-seven times." (Matthew 18:21–22)

Young Patrick was kidnapped from England and sold as a slave in Ireland. How amazing that he eventually went back and worked successfully for Ireland's conversion to Christianity! He truly practiced forgiveness. Do you have any place in your life where you need to practice forgiveness?

"Christ, be with me, Christ before me, Christ
behind me,
Christ in me, Christ beneath me, Christ above
me. . . .
May your salvation, O Lord, be ever with us."
(Patrick)

For more: Read the parable that follows these verses in Matthew, chapter 18, to hear what could happen if we are not forgiving.

March 18

[God says,] You shall keep my statutes and my ordinances; by doing so one shall live. (Leviticus 18:5)

Laws can seem so restrictive, especially those that limit our activities. Laws help societies to operate in some order. The Law of God starts with the Ten Commandments. Do you know what they are?

God of justice, you have established the Law and sent Jesus to fulfill it for us. Please help me to understand why laws and commandments are so important in helping to keep me free.

For more: You can find the Ten Commandments in Exodus, chapter 20.

JOSEPH

When his mother Mary had been engaged to Joseph, but before they lived together, she was found to be with child from the Holy Spirit. (Matthew 1:18)

Joseph had to believe without having seen. His faith stands as a strong witness for us. He trusted that the movement of the Holy Spirit in his heart and dreams was real, and he consented to follow God's will. Have you taken time lately to listen for God in your life?

Holy One, Joseph really shows me what it means to be faithful. I pray that when I am tested in the little things of my life, my faith will be as strong as his.

For more: There is not much in the Bible about Joseph. Read Matthew 1:18—2:23 to find out a bit more.

VERNAL EQUINOX, SPRING

A new heart I will give you, and a new spirit I will put within you; and I will remove from your body the heart of stone and give you a heart of flesh. (Ezekiel 36:26)

Every one of us has times when we've messed up so much we think that even God can't forgive us. But that's never the case. God's grace can change our heart of stone. Have you admitted your sins to God and asked for the grace of forgiveness?

Holy God, it can be embarrassing to admit how stony my heart has become, even while I didn't notice. Please give me the grace to open my stony heart to you.

For more: Feeling badly about our sins can paralyze us. Read Matthew, chapter 9, to hear about Jesus' forgiveness.

For your name's sake, O Yahweh, pardon my guilt, for it is great. (Psalm 25:11)

As we approach Easter, we naturally begin to consider how incredibly unworthy we have been of the great love of Jesus that resulted in his death for our sake. The good news is that Jesus died for us in spite of our unworthiness! He died for the forgiveness of our sins, to take our guilt away. Take some time today to thank Jesus for this gift of extravagant love.

Dear God, thank you for your extravagant love for your people. My limited human heart can only guess at the greatness of your divine love for us. Don't let me take that love for granted.

For more: In Luke, chapter 22, read about the Last Supper and how Jesus told the Apostles that his blood was to be poured out for the forgiveness of sins.

March 22

We know that all things work together for good for those who love God, who are called according to his purpose. (Romans 8:28)

At times in our life when things are just not going our way, we can easily blame God. God never wills bad things for us. However, after events happen, experience and time show us that our best growth and maturity is often gained through our worst struggles. Is there a struggle you can offer up to God in trust today?

God of love, I am doing my best to love you, but when things go wrong, it gets hard. Today I offer up my struggles to you in the hope that you are seeing some value in them that I cannot yet see.

For more: Check out the story of Queen Esther in the Book of Esther (between Nehemiah and Job), to see an example of all things working for the good for a woman who loved God.

Return to me and I will return to you, says the Lord of hosts. But you say, "How shall we return?" (Malachi 3:7)

The prophets challenged the people of Israel continually with all kinds of warnings and instructions from God. The fact that our God is humble enough to wait for us to come around astonishes us. Have you strayed away from God? How will you return?

All-wise God, the problem for me is that I'm not certain that I was ever with you in the first place! I do believe in you, and I hope that I have been with you, but I'm not exactly sure where we stand. Please strengthen my faith in you.

For more: Malachi, chapter 3, lists a number of ways in which people stray from God.

March 24

So acknowledge today and take to heart that the Lord is God in heaven above and on the earth beneath; there is no other. (Deuteronomy 4:39)

We can have difficulty accepting an all-powerful and all-knowing God. Everything around us encourages us to do whatever we want. But the Scriptures are clear that God is the CEO of the whole of our existence. Spend some time today considering how great God must be!

Dear God, I can only imagine how you manage to be present to each of us and still watch over the entire world. Thank you for taking the time to create, support, and love me as you do.

For more: Psalm 8 is a helpful psalm for meditating on how great God is.

ANNUNCIATION

Then Mary said, "Here am I, the servant of the Lord; let it be with me according to your word." Then the angel departed from her. (Luke 1:38)

Mary is often called the first disciple of Christ because she had to believe in him even before he was born. Her great faith gives us a model of true devotion. Are you willing to put your whole life in God's hands the way Mary did?

Dear God, my life is just beginning, and I'm afraid that if I put it in your hands, it might not be as exciting as I'd like it to be. Please help me to see how exciting and challenging a life of faith in you can be.

For more: To learn how to live a more faithful life, read the First Letter of Peter.

March 26

Yahweh is merciful and forgiving, slow to anger, rich in [steadfast] love. (Psalm 103:8)

Steadfast love seems like a contradiction in our flexible culture, yet our God is a God of steadfast love. God never gives up, and God has a good temper. We are blessed! Reflect today on how blessed you are to know the love of God.

Dear God, at times I know that what I do must really annoy you, or at least disappoint you. Thank you for being so merciful and for loving me through those times.

For more: Jesus gave an example of God's great love in the story of the prodigal son (Luke 15:11–32).

Just so, I tell you, there will be more joy in heaven over one sinner who repents than over ninety-nine righteous persons who need no repentance. (Luke 15:7)

Nobody is perfect. It's an old saying, but it seems to be one that we tend to forget. In each one of us are places where we know we fall short of God's great hopes for us. Examine your life today and offer God those areas where you need the most healing or conversion.

Holy Friend, thank you for loving us so much that you continually call us back to you. Direct me in my life today so that I can become that one repentant sinner.

For more: In Luke, chapter 15, the Pharisees are grumbling about whom Jesus hangs around with, and Jesus tells them a parable that ends with verse 7.

March 28

Six days you shall do your work, but on the seventh day you shall rest. (Exodus 23:12)

The command to rest at least once a week is repeated throughout the Hebrew Scriptures, reminding us that we must take care of ourselves if we are to truly serve God. It is possible to get so busy that we forget what is truly important—like God, for example! Even if you cannot take a whole day off, make sure you make time to rest this week.

God of peace, at times I feel so tired that I do forget you. Please forgive me for getting so wrapped up in busyness. Thank you for calling us to care for ourselves as we serve you.

For more: In Matthew 11:25–30, Jesus promises us rest, but not in the way we think.

So when you are offering your gift at the altar, if you remember that your brother or sister has something against you, leave your gift there before the altar and go; first be reconciled to your brother or sister, and then come and offer your gift. (Matthew 5:23–24)

Many of us would have to leave church on Sunday if we lived by these words. Yet Jesus has challenged us to put the community first and to make sure we are at peace with those around us. Do you need to be reconciled with someone in your life?

God of forgiveness, it is so much easier to talk with you about reconciling with my sister or brother than to actually go to her or him and work it out! Please be with me as I work to bring peace to the relationships in my life.

For more: Matthew 18:15–20 gives us a formula for when and how to confront someone when we know that something is not right in our relationship.

March 30

O Lord, hear; O Lord, forgive; O Lord, listen and act and do not delay! For your own sake, O my God, because your city and your people bear your name! (Daniel 9:19)

Reading the prophets is good for us because it reminds us that God does, on occasion, get angry with us. This prayer is the prayer of Daniel for Israel, asking for God's mercy because Israel has tried God's patience one time too many. Are you pushing the limit with God these days?

Dear God, I never really considered that your patience could run out. I suppose I was trying to hide behind my age so that I wouldn't have to be responsible for my actions. Please help me to own my behavior and to live according to your way.

For more: Read Genesis 19:24–29 to find out what happens when God's patience reaches its limits.

Now when the people complained in the hearing of the Lord about their misfortunes, the Lord heard it and his anger was kindled. (Numbers 11:1)

Even during the time of Moses, whining was a problem. It got on God's nerves; it got on Moses' nerves. In this particular case, it even got the people what they wanted. But the problem with whining is that it never seems to end. Have you been whining lately?

Dear God, sometimes I whine to get attention, and other times I truly don't realize that I'm whining at all. Please help me to put this childish habit aside and to learn to ask for my needs respectfully and maturely.

For more: The story of the flight of the Israelites from Egypt teaches us a lot about how God relates to us. Read this one small part of it in Numbers, chapter 11.

APRIL FOOLS' DAY

Even fools who keep silent are considered wise; when they close their lips, they are deemed intelligent. (Proverbs 17:28)

Even on April Fools' Day, the Bible has something to say to us. We are challenged throughout the Book of Proverbs to the better virtues, and today we are cautioned to keep silent rather than get carried away by trying to look wise. Make an honest effort to do more listening than talking today, and see what happens.

Dear God, sometimes I feel like a fool when my mouth gets going ahead of my brain. Please give me the good sense to know when to speak and when to keep silent.

For more: Read what Saint Paul tells the Corinthians about being fools for Christ in First Corinthians, chapter 4.

Now there was a great wind, so strong that it was splitting mountains and breaking rocks in pieces before the Lord, but the Lord was not in the wind. (1 Kings 19:11)

Elijah was waiting for God, and all the wild things that he thought were God, weren't. Because he was patient, Elijah finally did have an encounter, but in a surprising way. Keep your eyes open for God in the small, commonplace moments of your day today.

Dear God, I want you to come to me in a burning bush or a rainbow or in some other spectacular way. Help me to appreciate the little ways you show yourself to me every single day.

For more: To find out how Elijah did find God, read First Kings, chapter 19.

April 3

But [Moses] said, "O my Lord, please send someone else." (Exodus 4:13)

If we know about Moses at all, we tend to think of him as a great leader who brought the Israelites out of slavery in Egypt into the Promised Land. In the beginning Moses wasn't too sure about all of it. He tried to get a substitute. Are you trying to get a sub for the work God has chosen for you?

Dear God, like Moses I sometimes believe that your expectations of me are a little higher than what I am capable of. Please help me to trust that you will provide all that I need to do your will, if I just follow it.

For more: The prophet Jeremiah had similar doubts. Read Jeremiah, chapter 1, to hear God's response to this young, doubting messenger.

When you are praying, do not heap up empty phrases as the Gentiles do; for they think that they will be heard because of their many words. (Matthew 6:7)

One thing that keeps some of us from praying is not knowing the "right" thing to say. Jesus spoke a lot about praying, but the only formula he gave us was the Lord's Prayer—perhaps that's because he wants us to speak from our own hearts.

Kind God, I memorized prayers as a child, but they don't seem to apply to me now. I don't always know how to put what I am feeling into words. Help me to be comfortable offering those feelings to you anyway.

For more: Read Luke 18:9–14 to hear a parable about sincere prayer.

April 5

Then the Lord God will wipe away the tears from all faces, and the disgrace of his people he will take away from all the earth, for the Lord has spoken. (Isaiah 25:8)

On the day of final salvation, we will be reunited with everyone we know who has gone ahead of us to heaven. In the meantime we are called to trust that they are safe with God. Is there someone you need to let go of so you can get on with your life?

Living God, I would feel a lot better about letting go of (name) if I knew for certain that he or she is with you. Help me to let go and trust that my life can go on without this person because you are holding him or her in the palm of your hand.

For more: Isaiah, chapter 49, reminds us that we truly are held in the palm of God's own hand.

At the command of the Lord they would camp, and at the command of the Lord they would set out. They kept the charge of the Lord, at the command of the Lord by Moses. (Numbers 9:23)

A modern myth seems to be that a day will come when we no longer are subject to anyone else's commands. The truth is, that day never comes. All our life we submit to laws and authority, especially if we take seriously the word of God. Are you studying the word of God so that you will be able to freely submit to it?

All-wise God, I always believed that once I got my independence from my parents, I would be free to do whatever I pleased. Now I realize that freedom has limits and responsibilities attached to it. Help me to study your word so that I can become a responsible Christian adult.

For more: Check out Luke 22:39–46, about a time when even Jesus submitted to God's will.

JOHN BAPTIST DE LA SALLE (1651–1719)

Let the little children come to me; do not stop them; for it is to such as these that the kingdom of God belongs. (Mark 10:14)

Today we celebrate the feast of John Baptist de La Salle, who spent his life establishing schools for needy children throughout France. He is the patron of all teachers and the founder of the Brothers of the Christian Schools, who carry on his educational work throughout the world today. His dying words were, "I adore in all things the will of God in my regard."

Compassionate God, so often we do not understand your will in our life. It doesn't seem to make sense. Help us to trust you, as did John Baptist de La Salle, so that we can echo his words at the end of our life.

The joy that you give me is much greater than the joy of those who have an abundance of grain and wine. (Psalm 4:7)

There is a gladness that far surpasses the happiness that comes from good food and drink. It is a joy that is planted by God, and nothing or no one can take that away. How do you experience God's joy within you?

O God, you have put gladness in my heart. Let me not focus too much on all the things that are getting me down. Let my face reflect the joy of your presence within me.

DIETRICH BONHOEFFER (1906–1945)

Blessed are those who are persecuted for righteousness' sake, for theirs is the kingdom of heaven. (Matthew 5:10)

Dietrich Bonhoeffer was a German Lutheran theologian who spoke out early against the policies of Hitler's Nazi regime. Eventually he was hanged in a concentration camp for conspiring to assassinate Hitler. His friends had helped him escape Germany, but he felt that he had to return. He simply could not stand by, as so many others did, while so much injustice was taking place. Bonhoeffer once said, "Grace is *costly* because it calls us to follow, and it is *grace* because it calls us to follow *Jesus Christ.* It is costly because it costs a [person] his [or her] life, and it is grace because it gives a [person] the only true life."

God, it is so easy to turn the other way, to pretend that we do not see the injustice in our world. Help me to have the courage it takes to do the right thing, to stand up for righteousness' sake.

Then he poured water into a basin and began to wash the disciples' feet. (John 13:5)

Let's face it, feet can be stinky and sweaty and ugly. Even so, every Holy Thursday many congregations re-enact Jesus' act of washing his disciples' feet. This symbolic act is really quite powerful: God loves every part of us, even our stinky, sweaty, ugly parts, and he loves them enough to clean them. But before God can clean them, we have to be willing to show them to God. Do we try to hide the ugly parts of our soul from God?

God, I want you to know all parts of me and of my heart. Help me to trust you enough to let you wash my feet.

For more: Reconciliation is about showing our feet to God. Read Luke 5:12–16.

April 11

Since all have sinned and fall short of the glory of God, they are now justified by his grace as a gift, through the redemption which is in Christ Jesus. (Romans 3:23–24)

All of us sin and fall short of the glory of God—every single one of us. Nevertheless we are blessed by God's love and salvation through Jesus Christ. This is quite amazing when you think about it. We have not earned God's love. Through sin we have done quite the opposite. We have been given salvation anyway, an unwarranted gift of God's love. That's something we should be thankful for every single day.

God of all life, I know that I am a sinner, and yet you still love me. Thank you for your gift of salvation.

For more: Read Psalm 51, the prayer of a sinner.

We . . . boast in our sufferings, knowing that suffering produces endurance, and endurance produces character, and character produces hope, and hope does not disappoint us, because God's love has been poured into our hearts through the Holy Spirit which has been given to us. (Romans 5:3–5)

Bad things happen to good people all the time. When bad things happen to us, it is never easy to understand. Paul tells us that we should rejoice in our sufferings, for they lead to hope and bring us closer to God. If you have ever experienced suffering, this might ring true for you. God does not send suffering to test us, but God is with us in our suffering. God can bring about good in all situations. Suffering can lead to endurance, character, and hope that are grounded in God's love and the Holy Spirit. Next time you find yourself in a painful situation, ask yourself how God is working in that situation.

God, I know that you are with me always and can turn bad into good. May I always be aware of your presence and goodness in every situation.

For more: The Book of Job is about a good man who suffers a great deal. Read it and find out how he finds God.

April 13

The Spirit of God dwells in you. (Romans 8:9)

In certain parts of Asia, people greet each other by bowing and saying, "The divine in me celebrates the divine in you." How often do you see yourself and others as having God living inside? Is it possible to spend your day looking for the divine in everyone? Will that change how you see some people?

Loving God, I am honored by the gift of your Spirit that lives in me and in all people. May I always look to see your presence.

For more: Read John, chapter 14, especially from verse 18 to the end.

We have gifts that differ according to the grace given to us. (Romans 12:6)

What are your gifts and talents, the things that you do or know very well? We all have them, for they are given by God to us all. How are you nurturing your gifts? How are you using them for the glory of God and for God's people? Is there something you could be doing better?

Giver of all gifts, may I be grateful for my special gifts and use them for the good in every way.

For more: Read in Romans, chapter 12, about the Body of Christ. We all have different roles to play.

April 15

To each is given the manifestation of the Spirit for the common good. (1 Corinthians 12:7)

To each is given their own special gifts. What gifts do your friends have that you don't have? How about your parents, your teachers, or even those people you don't particularly like? Have you personally benefited or grown from the gifts of others? Are groups that you belong to better because of some of those gifts? We are all given specific gifts to use for the common good. How have you grown from someone else sharing their gifts?

Giver of all gifts, may I be grateful for the special gifts that other people have been given, and for the contributions they have made to my life.

For more: Read all of the twelfth chapter of the First Letter of Paul to the Corinthians.

April 16

The body does not consist of one member but of many. (1 Corinthians 12:14)

We each have been given our special gifts of the Holy Spirit needed to build up the Body of Christ. One person's gift cannot stand on its own. The most talented quarterback in the world is nothing without a sure-handed wide receiver. The best conductor has no purpose without an orchestra. Our gifts need to be connected to the gifts of other people. The building of the Body of Christ needs teamwork. How are your gifts connected to others? How many other people do your gifts connect you to?

I know, God, that I am a member of the Body of Christ. I thank you for all the members and for the ways in which we are all connected in the sharing of our gifts.

For more: Read the healing story in Luke 5:17–26. The paralyzed person could not have walked without teamwork.

SOJOURNER TRUTH (C. 1797–1883)

Blessed are they who maintain justice, who do what is right at all times! (Psalm 106:3)

Born a slave, Sojourner Truth gained her freedom and spent the rest of her life struggling to free slaves and to liberate other women. Motivated by deep Christian convictions, she confronted people with their racism, sexism, fears, and selfishness. She told a crowd: "Look at my arm! . . . I could work as much and eat as much as a man—when I could get it—and bear the lash as well! And ain't I a woman? I have borne thirteen children, and seen them most all sold to slavery, and when I cried out with my mother's grief, none but Jesus heard me! And ain't I a woman!"

God, give me the strength of Sojourner Truth to act justly and to struggle for the human rights of all people: women and men, children and elders, people of all races and backgrounds. And help us to create a world where all people are free from every kind of slavery.

The Lord does not see as mortals see; they look on the outward appearance, but the Lord looks on the heart. (1 Samuel 16:7)

Think about first impressions. They're based mainly on appearance, aren't they? We often judge others initially by how they look. How many times have you formed a false impression of someone? How many people have you written off because you didn't like what you saw?

O God, it is so good to know that you go deeper than our outward appearance. Our society places so much value on what we look like. You focus on what is in our hearts. Keep our hearts close to you.

For more: To learn more about how God chose David, see First Samuel, chapter 16.

April 19

Surely the Lord is in this place—and I did not know it. (Genesis 28:16)

In this story from the Old Testament, Jacob has this realization after a dream. It is a profound insight: there is no place where God is not present. How would you act differently if you really believed that God is always present with you wherever you are?

God-with-me, let me make Jacob's words my prayer, for I am always in your holy presence. Give me the gift of realizing that you are indeed present in this place, now, and in every place, always.

One who forgives an affront fosters friendship, but one who dwells on disputes will alienate a friend. (Proverbs 17:9)

Holding a grudge can be a disaster in a relationship. Forgiving a friend who has hurt us frees us from the burden of carrying a grudge that only gets heavier as time goes on. How has the refusal to forgive a friend affected both you and the relationship?

O God, it is so easy to alienate friends by refusing to forgive them, yet it is in the very act of forgiving that we are forgiven and that we help to bring about your Reign. Grant me a forgiving heart, and let me put my good intentions into acts of forgiveness.

April 21

I call all day, my God, but you never answer; all night long I call and cannot rest. (Psalm 22:2)

When is the last time you felt this way? Sometimes God seems so far away. We long for an answer, a response, but there isn't one. Jesus cries out these words from the cross. These feelings of being abandoned happen to all of us. Oddly enough though, these feelings help us realize how much God means to us.

O God, why is it that at times you seem to turn the other way? Even Jesus, your Son, felt abandoned on the cross. Give me the faith to outlast times of despair and loss.

EARTH DAY

Let the earth bless the Lord; let it sing praise to him and highly exalt him forever. (Daniel 3:74)

We often refer to the earth as our mother, and yet often we do not treat her with much respect or concern. The earth is our home, given to us by God. The earth reflects the fullness and wonder of God. Spend some time today thanking God for the wonders of the earth.

O Creator, you have given us this marvelous place we call Earth. Thank you for the gift of the earth and all its wonders. May I always treat the earth with respect, for it reflects your glory and fullness.

For more: Read the entire song in Daniel 3:52–90.

April 23

Now to God who is able to strengthen you according to my gospel and the proclamation of Jesus Christ . . . to whom be the glory forever! (Romans 16:25–27)

At times we feel as if no one understands us, or no one wants to understand us. During these times—and we all have them—we can find strength if we open ourselves up to God. While God is amazing—beyond all human understanding—God is also love, and God loves us deeply. Nowhere is this more clear than in the Gospels and in the story of Jesus Christ. In our darkest times, God can give us strength and the knowledge that we are never alone. Have you ever experienced that?

When I am feeling alone, I want to turn to you and find strength in you, O God. May I never be afraid to put my trust in you.

For more: Read the story of Shadrach, Meshach, and Abednego found in the third chapter of Daniel. They put their trust in God when life looked bleak, and were not disappointed.

Do not lag in zeal, be ardent in spirit, serve the Lord. (Romans 12:11)

Faith is not just something we have. It's something we have to be attentive to and work at. Faith is not a possession, it is action. When is the last time you had zeal or energy for your faith, your prayer life, or your church? In these busy times, how can we keep our excitement and remain aglow with the Spirit in order to serve God?

May I be aware of the Spirit inside me, Holy Friend. Help me to be alive with your Spirit so that I may better serve you.

For more: Read about the first time the church received the gift of the Spirit, found in Acts of the Apostles, chapter 2.

April 25

Do not follow your base desires, but restrain your appetites. (Sirach 18:30)

It's all about self-control, isn't it? We need to keep our desires for more possessions, for revenge, for unlimited pleasure in check, and restraining our appetite goes way beyond limiting what we eat. How well do you practice self-control? Where do you want to do better?

O God, it is so easy to give in to temptation, but we know that we become stronger by resisting those things that diminish us. Help me to be strong and to fight the good fight. I need the grace of self-control.

Your love, Yahweh, reaches to heaven. . . . Your people find refuge in the shelter of your wings. (Psalm 36:5–7)

What a wonderful image: to be safe in the shelter of God's wings. God's precious, steadfast love extends to all people. All are welcome to seek refuge in God.

O God, you remind us in many ways of your constant love and care for us. Help me to take refuge in you when I need to soar and feel supported. How precious is your steadfast love, O God.

April 27

All one's ways may be pure in one's own eyes, but the Lord weighs the spirit. (Proverbs 16:2)

This proverb helps keep us honest. We may think that we have pure motives when we help people in need, for instance. But few of us have completely pure motives. There always seems to be some ulterior motive. Thankfully God looks past our ways to the depths of our heart, and gives us grace to keep trying.

O God, help me to be single-hearted in my ways and deeds, for no matter what, you know what is in my heart. Let me act with both spirit and heart set on doing what's right and good.

We walk by faith, not by sight. (2 Corinthians 5:7)

At times in our life, we do not understand why something is happening the way it is, and later, sometimes many years later, we are able to look back and make sense of it all. This is what it means to walk by faith: to go on with life when we do not understand why things are happening the way they are. When we walk forward into the unknown, trusting in God's help, even if we do it hesitantly, we are walking by faith. We are trusting that God will care for us. Have you had times in your life when this has happened? Is it happening now? Has it made your faith stronger?

Loving God, thank you for the gift of faith that carries me forward in spite of my doubts. Strengthen my faith.

For more: Joseph had faith when he took Mary for his wife. Read about it in Matthew 1:18–25.

CATHERINE OF SIENA

Truly I tell you, just as you did it to one of the least of these who are members of my family, you did it to me. (Matthew 25:40)

Catherine of Siena lived during a time of conflict between dozens of Italian city-states and a time of leadership problems in the church. She mediated between warring cities, ministered to sick people, and was a mystic, someone unusually close to God. She was later named a doctor of the Catholic church. She once said, "As we understand, so we love, and when we love, we find ourselves united with the transformed in love." Like Catherine we are called to work every day toward a better relationship with and understanding of God.

Dear God, thank you for giving us great women like Catherine to show us that you are real and to remind us that our desires can never really match what you long to give us.

For more: Catherine gave a great deal of energy to serving poor people. Read Matthew 25:31–46 to hear why that's a good idea for all Christians.

Many have fallen by the edge of the sword, but not as many as have fallen because of the tongue. (Sirach 28:18)

We all know how awful we feel when we become aware of a rumor that has been going around about us. Funny how we still manage to pass along rumors about others, even though we are sometimes unsure just how true they really are. Do rumors die with you, or do you pass them along?

Dear God, sharing rumors about people can be exciting—until the rumor is about us. Help me to remember that I wouldn't want people talking about me. Help me so that I can refuse to spread stories and to check in with the actual person instead.

For more: Read Matthew 16:13–20 to hear about a time when Jesus asked the disciples, "Who do they say that I am?" and then stopped the rumor.

May 1

Avoid stupid controversies, genealogies, dissensions, and quarrels about the law, for they are unprofitable and worthless. (Titus 3:9)

Many passages in the Scriptures caution us to watch what we say and how we say it. Here we are warned against word battles of any kind. Better to keep silent. Try to avoid any kind of word battle, quarrel, or bickering all day, even if you're just listening to it.

God of peace, some of us are good at word battles, and others just provide the audience. Either way I don't want to be spending my time and energy on unprofitable and worthless things. Give me the strength to walk away when I'm tempted to join in.

For more: Read the Letter to Titus to learn how to be a good disciple and how to preach the word of God through your actions.

Now the Lord said to Abram, "Go from your country and your kindred and your father's house to the land that I will show you." (Genesis 12:1)

Abram (Abraham) lived even before we had a name for the one God whom we now know as Father, Son, and Holy Spirit; or Creator, Redeemer, and Sanctifier. Even so, Abram and Sarah, his wife, demonstrated great faith by following the prompting of this unknown God in their hearts and leaving everything they knew. Would you recognize the voice of God in your heart?

Holy One, I feel many things in my heart from day to day, but I do find it hard to figure out if any of it is actually from you. Please help me sort through my inner understandings so that I can recognize your voice in my life.

For more: Read Genesis, chapters 18 and 21, to see how Sarah laughed when God told her she would have a child as an old woman. But she did, so she named him Laughter (Isaac).

May 3

Speak to all the congregations of the people of Israel and say to them: You shall be holy, for I the Lord your God am holy. (Leviticus 19:2)

Each of us has a call to holiness: that is, to imitate Christ to the best of our ability. Some people give their life to church ministries, but most of us try to be Christlike in business, with our families, in the ordinary life we live. No matter how we live our life, God calls us to be holy. Would you describe yourself as holy?

Dear God, I can think of many words to describe myself, but I would be nervous to include *holy* on the list. I always thought that *holy* meant "perfect," but now I know that is not true. Help me to find the path that will lead me to the holiness you have planned for me.

For more: Read Colossians, chapter 1, to hear how Christ has interceded for us so that we can be "holy and blameless and irreproachable before him."

For God is not unjust; he will not overlook your work and the love that you showed for his sake in serving the saints, as you still do. (Hebrews 6:10)

God pays attention to even the smallest act of kindness that we do. We can get so wrapped up in trying to hide our failings that we forget how pleased and happy God becomes when we love one another. Take some time today to do something good for someone—something that only God can see.

Dear God, thank you for taking pleasure in my attempts to bring joy to the world. I am grateful for your love and attention. Guide me more and more toward you and away from those things that displease you.

For more: Read Hebrews, chapter 6, to hear the message of hope written at a time when the Jewish and the Gentile followers of Jesus were not getting along too well.

May 5

An educated person knows many things, and one with much experience knows what he is talking about. (Sirach 34:9)

As we learn from our education and experiences, we gain confidence and maturity. If we consult them, they help us to cope with the stresses of life and to respond creatively. Have you thanked your parents or God lately for the great privilege of your education and your life experiences?

Living God, I do not always enjoy the pressures of my education, but I am sometimes surprised at how much I have learned. Thank you for the gift of my intelligence and for the patience of my parents, friends, and teachers.

For more: Check out John, chapter 17, to see how Jesus prayed for the disciples when he knew that he had to leave them, just like your teachers and mentors pray for you when you leave for a new challenge.

HENRY DAVID THOREAU (1817–1862)

And after [Jesus] had dismissed the crowds, he went up the mountain by himself to pray. (Matthew 14:23)

Henry David Thoreau embraced caring for the earth and finding God in nature long before they became popular. For twenty-six months he lived alone at Walden Pond in order to "live deliberately, to front only the essential facts of life, and see if I could not learn what it had to teach, and not, when I came to die, discover that I had not lived." Are you willing to spend time alone with God, to face yourself, and to examine your values?

God, our creator, spending time alone can be scary for me. It seems as though I am missing out on part of life. Help me to see that taking time to speak with you is checking in to the most important part of life.

For more: Matthew, chapter 6, lists a number of practices that will help us to grow as Christians. Check out verses 5 and 6 on praying alone.

Know then in your heart that as a parent disciplines a child so the Lord your God disciplines you. (Deuteronomy 8:5)

The word *discipline* means that we accept the role of a "disciple," a learner or follower. This verse reminds us that God wants us to be disciples of our parents. On top of that, we are called to be God's disciples. Our human desire for independence fights against discipline, and we don't want to submit to it. The next time someone offers you discipline, or you have to discipline yourself (follow what you know is the right way), take a moment to thank God for this person's faithfulness and for your own wisdom.

God, our loving parent, I like to do things my way, in my own time, and I get frustrated when discipline stops me. Please help me to see that discipline helps to mold me into a faithful adult.

For more: Read Deuteronomy, chapter 8, which reminds us not to forget God when things are going well for us.

You must understand this, my beloved: let everyone be quick to listen, slow to speak, slow to anger. (James 1:19)

All through the Bible, we are cautioned about the power of words and the tongue. Over and over in both the Hebrew Scriptures and the Christian Testament, we are taught to watch our words. Have your words caused trouble recently? If so, what might you do to reconcile matters?

Holy Wisdom, thank you for the gifts of speech and communication, which are so important as I learn to relate to the world. Please help me to remember the power of the words I say so that I say them carefully, that is, full of care.

For more: The Letter of James starts with a whole chapter on how to act on God's word instead of being a passive listener. Read the first chapter, and underline verses that stand out to you.

May 9

[Jesus] said to them, "Why are you afraid? Have you still no faith?" (Mark 4:40)

Trusting in Jesus takes a great deal of faith. After all, we cannot see him or meet him physically. But we can meet him in the Scriptures and in prayer. Jesus wants to walk with us through every moment of our life, but we need to invite him in so that fear goes away. Offer up a fear of yours to Jesus. Put faith in Jesus in the place of fear.

Christ, our help, I wish I could have met you in person, but then I wonder if I would have doubted you like the disciples did. Please help me to trust that with you in my life, I have no need to fear.

For more: Read Mark 4:35–41 to get the whole story on how the disciples doubted Jesus.

Then Moses answered, "But suppose they do not believe me or listen to me, but say, 'The Lord did not appear to you.'" (Exodus 4:1)

When God first asked Moses to help free the Israelites from slavery, Moses wasn't too sure about the whole thing. He made a lot of excuses. When we feel the hand of God in our life, sometimes we do the same thing. Make a decision today about something you've been putting off by making excuses.

Holy Friend, I feel I'm ready to make my own decisions, but sometimes I'm not sure that I have the best or even enough information to move ahead. I put this decision in your hands, and I pray that you will lead me to right action. (Mention your decision.)

For more: Read Luke 9:51–62 to see a time when Jesus got tired of people making excuses.

May 11

Be careful then how you live, not as unwise people but as wise. (Ephesians 5:15)

If we take our faith seriously, we take on a whole new task of living a Christlike life. We are called by Christ to be models of right action and wisdom for those around us. Wisdom means that we try to consider the consequences of our actions, that we seek advice about how to make decisions, and that we pay attention to people's needs. Consider your lifestyle right now. Are you living wisely?

Holy God, I would like to live a new life in you, but I like the flexibility to do what I want. Search my heart and help me find the path that brings me the greatest joy while I grow still wiser and closer to you.

For more: Read Ephesians, chapters 5 and 6, to hear what a Christlike life entails.

You protect the simplehearted; when I was brought low, you saved me. (Psalm 116:6)

When we consider our life, we start to realize how often we have come through difficult times when we really weren't paying attention. Simple as we can sometimes be, God continually watches out for us. Take a few moments today and thank God for pulling you through a tough time.

Compassionate God, thank you for supporting and defending me the way you do. I promise to try to trust you more as I set my sights on following you.

For more: Read Psalm 116 out loud, slowly, and consider how much God really loves you.

May 13

And Jesus said to them, "Follow me." . . . And immediately they left their nets and followed him. (Mark 1:17–18)

Sometimes deciding to follow Christ takes a long time. We labor over the decision, seriously considering the consequences. Other times it is immediate and spontaneous. We simply know what is right to do. If Jesus came up to you today and said, "Follow me," how would you answer?

Creator of the universe, knowing about you is one thing, but making a decision to actually follow you takes a lot more commitment. Help me to trust completely, like Jesus' first disciples, and immediately to let go of my prejudices or pet projects so that I can follow you.

For more: Read Luke, chapter 9, to find out how Jesus instructed the disciples once they decided to follow him.

Finally, beloved, whatever is true, whatever is honorable, whatever is just, whatever is pure, whatever is pleasing, whatever is commendable, if there is any excellence and if there is anything worthy of praise, think about these things. (Philippians 4:8)

Because of the Internet and the World Wide Web, we have access to enormous amounts of information. Christians are challenged to focus attention on those things that lead to a closer relationship with God. Take time today to think about what is true, honorable, just, pure, pleasing, and commendable in your life: yes, believe that your life has these elements.

All-wise God, I do understand that limiting my input can lead me closer to you, but I also have a great hunger and thirst for knowledge. Thank you for the gift of my brain and intelligence. Help me to use it in ways that glorify you and serve the human family.

For more: Read Philippians, chapter 4, where the gifts that Paul affirms in the Philippians serve as examples for us.

May 15

I have called you by name, you are mine. (Isaiah 43:1)

A wise woman once said, "What I do is expendable, who I am is not." God does not love us because we get good grades or set records for the track team or have the best voice. If that were the case, what would happen when we failed a test or came in second or were too sick to sing? God loves us—period. Each of us has been called by God to be with God, both in this life and in the next. God wants to be with us. God loves us for who we are; do you love yourself for who you are?

Thank you, God, for your unconditional love for me. May I always recognize that love.

For more: Take a look at the story of the prodigal son (Luke 15:11–32). It's about a parent's unconditional love.

I have indeed received much joy and encouragement from your love. (Philemon 1:7)

When friends are having a hard time or are in the midst of a crisis, we often have a difficult time figuring out what to say. At these times this passage can be helpful. Sometimes all people need or want is our presence. Just being there as a loving friend is enough. Could someone in your life use your presence?

Loving God, help me to see the people who are in need of my presence.

For more: When Jesus was carrying his cross, many of his friends walked with him. Read about it in Luke 23:26–29.

May 17

Build yourselves up on your most holy faith. (Jude 1:20)

We spend a lot of time in our society building up our body, but how many of us actually devote any time or energy to building up our faith? Just like our body, our faith thrives when we focus on it and set aside time to build it up. Do you build up your body? Do you build up your faith?

God of all life, may I be as concerned with my faith as I am with my body and its appearance.

For more: Before Jesus was turned over to Pilate, he spent time building up his faith in preparation for the coming ordeal. See Luke 22:39–46 or Mark 14:32–42.

He said to her, "Daughter, your faith has made you well; go in peace, and be healed of your disease." (Mark 5:34)

Curing and healing are different experiences. Sometimes Jesus cured people, but mostly he healed them. A cure in the body can still leave a scarred soul. Healing involves our mind and our soul. Do you have a hurt in your mind or your soul that you can give to the Divine Healer in faith today?

Healer of us all, there are some things in me that I think even you cannot heal. Please give me the courage and faith to hand them over to you so that I can be whole.

For more: Read Mark 5:21–34 to get the whole story on this woman who learned that Jesus wants a healing relationship, not just a chance for a curing touch.

Jesus himself stood among them and said to them, "Peace be with you." (Luke 24:36)

When someone we love dies, we feel a lot of pain. In fact, if the person was close enough to us, sometimes we feel like part of us died with them. Imagine how enlivened the Apostles felt when they saw for themselves that Jesus really was alive and was bringing peace to them. Have you allowed the peace of Jesus into your heart to help with your losses?

God who is with us, thank you for bringing the gift of peace into my life, especially when I am feeling the saddest and most empty. Help me to keep my heart open so that I can experience that peace when I most need it.

For more: Find John, chapter 14, and read Jesus' words of reassurance to his disciples.

I will praise you, Yahweh, with my whole heart; I will proclaim your wonderful works. (Psalm 9:1)

When we pray for something and don't get it, it is easy to be angry with God. When we do receive what we have prayed for, we often move along to ask for something else right away. Today take some time to remember that God's ways are often mysterious, but that God always desires good for us.

Holy One, thank you for the many times that you have answered my prayers. Thank you too for the times when you did not give me what I wanted but led me to even better gifts.

For more: Read Psalm 9 aloud slowly.

Awe came upon everyone, because many wonders and signs were being done by the apostles. (Acts of the Apostles 2:43)

In the Book of Acts, we hear about what happened to Jesus' little band of Apostles after he had ascended into heaven. The love and peace of Jesus so filled their hearts that it overflowed from them, causing many wonders and signs. Does the love and peace of Jesus flow from you?

Dear God, when I was small, even simple things filled me with wonder, and the moments of awe seemed endless. Now I don't seem to find too much to get excited about. Please open my eyes so I can see your love and peace in the world and share it with others.

For more: Find Acts of the Apostles, chapter 2, and read about the descent of the Holy Spirit upon the disciples.

The steadfast love of the Lord never ceases; his mercies never come to an end. (Lamentations 3:22)

Another way to describe "lamentations" is "whining." Jeremiah is not too happy about the situation in which he has found himself, and he is whining to God, much like children whine to their parents. Yet in spite of his predicament, Jeremiah cannot help acknowledging the goodness of God. Today if you feel like whining, try to find something to be thankful for instead.

Patient God, even though I could find things to whine about today, I choose to concentrate on your blessings instead. Thank you for my life this day. Thank you for my family and my friends. Thank you for my education and my freedom.

For more: Check out Lamentations, chapter 3, to hear how Jeremiah continued to have faith.

May 23

[Jesus] sat down, called the twelve, and said to them, "Whoever wants to be first must be last of all and servant of all." (Mark 9:35)

Wanting to be the leader, the top dog, the person who gets the credit is only human. The Apostles were human too, and they argued about who was the greatest of them. In Jesus' day great people were waited on by servants, they did not serve. Jesus' answer did not really make sense. In order to be first, are you willing to put yourself at the service of others?

Servant of all, it really seems as though many paths lay ahead of me, and I want to be successful on at least one of them. Help me to realize that in serving others, I can learn the things I'll need to find real success in this world and in the next.

For more: Read Mark 9:33–37 to see who Jesus felt was truly important.

You shall keep my sabbaths and reverence my sanctuary: I am the Lord. (Leviticus 26:2)

Even back in the time of the Hebrew Scriptures, Leviticus, the book of the Law, instructed the people to keep one day holy in honor of God. These days we may have forgotten what that really means, and we use Sunday, our Sabbath, as just another free day. Many people have to work at their jobs on Sunday. Today make a commitment to get to church on Sundays.

Dear God, it is easy for me to find fault with church services and communities. There are hypocrites there, true. But help me to understand that the only hypocrite I need to be concerned with is myself, and that because we all are sinners, we all fit in the Body of Christ.

For more: Read Exodus 20:8–11 to find out where the teaching about keeping a Sabbath day of rest came from.

Now when they saw the boldness of Peter and John and realized that they were uneducated and ordinary men, they were amazed and recognized them as companions of Jesus. (Acts of the Apostles 4:13)

By education and by community standing are just two of the many ways we judge one another. When Jesus chose the Apostles, he looked at their hearts and their faithfulness, not at their external positions or training. Today take a second look at someone you have written off as a nobody.

Creator of all, if I had been alive right after Jesus died, I may have missed the message of salvation because I might have written off the messengers as nobodies. Please help me to realize that your messengers come from all walks of life.

For more: Check out Luke 24:13–35 to read about a time when Jesus' own disciples almost wrote him off.

I will put my spirit within you, and you shall live. (Ezekiel 37:14)

At times all of us feel that we have no hope left. God delights in bringing hope back into our life if we will only ask for it. Today invite God into a hopeless situation that you know about.

Dear God, sometimes my heart sinks, and I do feel hopeless and almost dead. I can't seem to find the motivation to even move. Be with me in those moments, and grant me the wisdom to realize that your Spirit can motivate me if I only ask.

For more: Check out Ezekiel 37:1–14 to hear one of the most famous graveyard stories in the Bible.

May 27

Now faith is the assurance of things hoped for, the conviction of things not seen. (Hebrews 11:1)

Faith is difficult to define because it concerns itself with hopes and things we cannot see. Being sure of our hopes and absolutely certain of what we cannot see may seem crazy, but faith is real. Today consider the stars on a cloudy night: you cannot see them, but they are still there.

Faithful God, thank you for the gift of faith and for the mind and heart you have given me to understand it. When I experience a moment of doubt, help me to remember the stars.

For more: Read Hebrews, chapter 11, to see the roots of our faith.

Every friend says, "I too am a friend"; but some friends are friends only in name. (Sirach 37:1)

Second to family, and sometimes before family, our friends have a lot of influence in our life. God made us relational people; we all need friends. Whether we have many or few, these friends can affect how we live our life. Take some time today to examine your friendships. Thank God for your true friends, and ask God's help to bring "friends only in name" around.

Dear God, if we are not supposed to judge, how can I decide which of my friends are true and which are false? My friends are my second family, and I trust them. Please give me the insight to recognize if I am hanging out with friends who are not true, and to celebrate the friends that are true.

For more: Sirach, chapter 37, gives a number of clues on how to recognize false friends and bad counselors.

May 29

But you will receive power when the Holy Spirit has come upon you; and you will be my witnesses . . . to the ends of the earth. (Acts of the Apostles 1:8)

Right before Jesus ascended into heaven, the Apostles were afraid. In fact they locked themselves in a room, even though Jesus gave them this encouragement. Can you think of a time when fear caused you to lock yourself away, physically or emotionally?

Holy Friend, as your Apostles believed, I want to believe in you, but at times I find it difficult and want to hide away. I would like to trust your word, but it doesn't seem to apply in my situation. Help me to stay open to the Spirit in times of fear so that I can feel your power in my life.

For more: Read Luke 12:22–34 to hear a longer passage on how we can deal with our fears.

JOAN OF ARC
(CA. 1412–1431)

I will pour out my spirit on all flesh; your sons and your daughters shall prophesy, your old . . . shall dream dreams and your young . . . shall see visions. (Joel 2:28)

When she was seventeen years old, Joan of Arc led the French troops to victory over an invading English army. Her inspiration came from heavenly voices, and she was faithful to her vision. Joan was captured by the enemy and accused of witchcraft, and was executed at the age of twenty. How much courage do you have to follow your convictions?

God of strength, grant me courage to live out the vision of the good life that you have planted in me. Help me to be strong in doing right in the face of opposition.

May 31

To him who is able to keep you from falling. (Jude 1:24)

When we are walking or running, we fall if we are careless or if we are paying attention to something else. The same is true as we walk on our spiritual path. It is easy to get distracted or sidetracked. Before we know it, we have fallen on our spiritual behinds by abandoning prayer or by engaging in unhealthy practices. But if we stay focused, God will keep us from falling, will guide us on the right path.

God, you are able to keep me from falling. I want to stay focused on you and your love.

For more: King Saul lost his focus. Read about his struggle with David in First Samuel, chapters 13–20.

Shout for joy to God, all the lands! (Psalm 100:1)

With June comes summer, and a time to relax and enjoy God's good earth. "Shout for joy" this summer by making the most of the leisurely days, and remember that each one is a gift from God.

Creator of the universe, as we begin summer, may I make the most of each day, whether I am recreating, working, or studying. Help me to truly shout for joy to you!

God shows no partiality. (Galatians 2:6)

We tend to think that God is on "our side" in most things. Christians tend to believe that God wants everyone to believe in Jesus. But God shows no partiality. We are all God's works of art. God loves Buddhist believers and faithful Muslims as much as God loves Christian people. God does not see people in groups. And God is not on the side of some people and not others. Are you?

May I accept all people, God, as your people whom you love.

For more: Jesus tried to "label" a woman, but she ended up changing his ministry once he saw her as a person. Read about it in Matthew 15:21–28.

There is no longer Jew or Greek, there is no longer slave or free, there is no longer male and female; for all of you are one in Christ Jesus. (Galatians 4:28)

In other words there is neither winner nor loser, there is neither insider nor outsider, there is neither gay nor straight; we are all one in Jesus Christ. It is easy to label people and put them into neat categories. But when we do this, we cease to see them as people. They become the category we have placed them in, adopting all the traits (usually negative) of that category. And yet we are told that there are no labels with Jesus. How often do you label people? Does it bother you to be labeled?

No label fits you, God. Help me to remove the labels from my mind and see people in all their uniqueness.

For more: Read the parable of the good Samaritan (Luke 10:25–37) about labels and overturning them.

June 4

For you were called to freedom; . . . only do not use your freedom as an opportunity for the flesh, but through love become slaves to one another. (Galatians 5:13)

One of the scariest things about being human is having the will to choose good over evil, or evil over good. We determine the kind of life that we will lead, and we have to redetermine it every single day, with every single decision. Only God's grace lets us make good choices. How are you exercising your freedom? Are you choosing to be a servant to others?

Loving God, it's hard to make good choices each time—to choose doing good—but I am grateful for the opportunity. Just keep your grace flowing so that I can choose well.

For more: See Luke 16:13—we cannot serve two masters.

The fruit of the Spirit is love, joy, peace, patience, kindness, generosity, faithfulness, gentleness, and self-control. (Galatians 5:22–23)

Choosing good over evil becomes extremely difficult when we can't tell the difference between the two. Thankfully the Scriptures give us guidelines for decision making. They give us a list to help us look for the presence of the Spirit. Does "option A" possess love, joy, or peace? Will choosing it bring about kindness, faithfulness, or gentleness in you or in anyone else? What about "option B"? Try applying these guidelines to some decision you need to make today.

Holy Wisdom, choosing the good is not always easy. First I have to find the good. Thank you for your Spirit, who helps me to find it.

For more: We're not the only ones who struggle. See Romans 7:14–23.

June 6

If we live by the Spirit, let us also be guided by the Spirit. (Galatians 5:25)

Choosing the good in the big decisions of our life is not all there is to making a good life. We want to arrive at the point where we habitually go for the good, even in small matters. If we become attuned to the Spirit—love, joy, peace, patience, kindness, generosity, faithfulness, gentleness, self-control—we begin to walk by the Spirit. Are you attuned to the Spirit? Do you walk by the Spirit?

I want to know your Spirit, gentle God, and learn to journey with the help of the Holy Spirit. Come, spirit of the living God.

For more: The Spirit is a powerful force. Read about its first appearance to the disciples (Acts of the Apostles, chapter 2) and the profound effect it had on them.

Bear one another's burdens. (Galatians 6:2)

We all have our own crosses to bear—some great and some small. So we ask ourselves, How am I supposed to help carry someone else's burdens when at times I feel like I can barely carry my own? We do know, however, that our own burdens feel much lighter when someone else helps us carry them. Has someone helped you carry your burdens? Could someone use your help with his or her burden?

God, thank you for the people who have helped me with my burdens over the years. Give me strength and guidance, that I may help others.

For more: Sometimes burdens can be literally heavy, like Simon's burden (Matthew 27:32, Mark 15:21, Luke 23:26). Could you have carried it?

So God created humankind in his image, in the image of God he created them; male and female he created them. (Genesis 1:27)

Is there a more profound description of human dignity anywhere? We are created in the very image of God, female and male. Look into the mirror and realize that you are gazing at an image of God. Go ahead, try it.

O God, forgive me my constant self-criticism. I get so caught up in "if only's": if only I was better looking or smarter or a better athlete. You created me in your image. Let me celebrate that today!

For more: Read Ephesians 2:10, in which Paul calls us God's work of art.

Wait for Yahweh; be strong, and let your heart take courage. Yes, wait for God! (Psalm 27:14)

Waiting is not easy. We tend to get impatient quickly. Do we have the patience to wait until we experience the presence of God? Isn't this what faith is all about? (Hint: We really don't have to wait long; God is right here, right now.)

Ever-present God, grant me patience, especially during those times when it seems that you are nowhere to be found. Give me a strong, courageous heart to wait for you, knowing that you are with me.

June 10

And on the seventh day God finished the work that he had done, and he rested on the seventh day from all the work that he had done. So God blessed the seventh day and hallowed it, because on it God rested from all the work that he had done in creation. (Genesis 2:2–3)

This is an interesting passage. Does God really need to rest? Or is the purpose of God's resting to teach us the importance of taking time out? How well do we "keep holy the Lord's day"? If God needed a day off, don't we need two?

God, our creator, you have shown us that resting is a sacred activity. Help me to view rest as a time to refresh my body and soul. Let me realize that rest is a blessing because it comes from you.

*Let another praise you, and not your own mouth—
a stranger, and not your own lips. (Proverbs 27:2)*

While it is important to have a positive self-image and to feel good about ourselves, few people appreciate a braggart. No one enjoys being around one. When someone gives you praise though, say "Thanks," because they have given you a gift. Who can you genuinely compliment today? Who could use some praise from you today?

God, thank you for the reminder that we should make a point of praising others and not expect to be praised ourselves. Help me to affirm the good that I see in those around me.

June 12

Listen, you that are deaf; and you that are blind, look up and see! (Isaiah 42:18)

It is easy to ignore a passage such as this because it does not apply to most of us. Or does it? In the Bible deafness and blindness are often used symbolically. What voices are we deaf to: persons we don't like? issues we would rather not hear about? How are we blind? What do we choose not to see or look at? The cure: Listen. Look up and see!

God, thank you for the gifts of hearing and sight. Help me to really listen and to really see. Open my ears and eyes to the needs of others and to your will.

In [Christ] the whole structure is joined together and grows into a holy temple in the Lord; in whom you also are built together spiritually into a dwelling place for God. (Ephesians 2:21–22)

We are dwelling places for the Spirit. Our God lives in each one of us. God knows our heart and our thoughts intimately. We are never alone, abandoned, orphaned. If God dwells within us, then God is part of us, and we cannot be without God. Therefore God shares our life with us—both the good and the bad, the significant and the simple. Our God loves us enough to want to be with us always.

Even though I may not always say it, God, I am happy that you love me and want to be with me.

For more: See Romans 8:9–11. The Spirit is in us!

June 14

Flee from sin as from a snake; for if you approach sin, it will bite you. Its teeth are lion's teeth, and can destroy human lives. (Sirach 21:2)

Most people are afraid of or at least careful around snakes, which is why the author of this passage uses the comparison. A poisonous snake will likely bite us if approached. Isn't sin like that? We can be "bitten" by sin, and the results of our sin can hurt ourselves and others. When has a sin you committed hurt others or destroyed a relationship?

God, forgive me for being so attracted to what can be dangerous for me. Help me to avoid temptation, and do not let sin overpower me so that I end up hurting others.

Now to him who by the power at work within us is able to accomplish abundantly far more than all we can ask or imagine, to him be glory. (Ephesians 3:20–21)

Our God lives with us through the Spirit, and with the Spirit we can do great things. When we get a good grade on an impossible test that we studied hard for, it's easy to forget that God gave us our brain and the ability to read and study. But more than that, God acts through us. When we are nice to the person who is having a horrible day, it is God working through us who is reaching out to that person. Not only does God live in us, God works through us.

God, help me to be an instrument for you, that you may better love your people through me.

For more: God does not always work through the big storm or the earthquake. See how God appears in 1 Kings 19:11–13.

June 16

Then [God] said to [Moses], "Come no closer! Remove the sandals from your feet, for the place on which you are standing is holy ground." (Exodus 3:5)

This famous scene from Exodus at the burning bush reminds us that where God is, is holy ground. So all ground is holy. God is everywhere present, so wherever we are, no matter what the circumstances, we are on holy ground, for we are in the presence of God. How do you feel about that?

Repeat this prayer slowly several times: "God is present, and where God is, is holy ground."

I . . . beg you to lead a life worthy of the calling to which you have been called. (Ephesians 4:1)

What are you being called to? This question is asking, What kind of person are you going to be? We are all called to live a Christian life as disciples of Jesus. That can take many forms. So when Paul is begging us to lead a life worthy of that calling, he is not necessarily asking us to choose to preach or to teach religion. Rather he is asking us to live lives that are worthy of the disciples of Jesus. Is your life worthy of the calling? With God's grace can you change things to make it more worthy?

Dear God, may I always be worthy of being called a "disciple of Jesus."

For more: To read more about the call, see the second chapter of James.

June 18

Bless the Lord, all that grows in the ground; sing praise to him and highly exalt him forever. (Daniel 3:76)

During this growing season of early summer, many people are tending their gardens and crops. Watching things grow is wonderful and inspiring. Spend some time today walking through a garden or a park or even examining a plant in your home. How do growing things give glory to God?

O God, our creator and the creator of all living and growing things, let me take time out during this growing season to appreciate the miracle of growth. Help me to grow as well, and by my growth to give glory to you.

Be angry but do not sin; do not let the sun go down on your anger. (Ephesians 4:26)

Our anger can scare us because it is such a strong emotion. We are often told that we shouldn't get angry. Jesus even tells us to turn the other cheek and to forgive our neighbor seventy times seven times. But anger is an emotion that occurs naturally; we just have it. Caught up in our anger, we shove aside forgiveness. This passage offers good advice: "Do not let the sun go down on your anger." Okay, you will become angry, but deal with your anger immediately. Write a nasty letter and then tear it up, exercise, talk it out, but don't go to bed angry. If it is allowed to fester, anger just eats us up.

Help me, God. I want to deal with my anger so that I may forgive others as you have forgiven me.

For more: See Matthew 5:21–26, where Jesus tells us not to come to the altar angry.

June 20

A good name is to be chosen rather than great riches. (Proverbs 22:1)

Given the choice, many of us might choose wealth over a "good name," and yet in the end, it is our good name that people will remember. How can you strive to be a better person, to be someone that others respect and look up to? How can you strengthen your good name?

O God, riches and wealth are so tempting because we can get so many things with money. Help me to focus on being a person whose riches are internal and whose reputation is priceless. Let my good name reflect your goodness.

Let no evil talk come out of your mouth. (Ephesians 4:29)

Have you ever engaged in evil talk: spreading half-truths about someone to hurt them? using racial slurs? telling someone lies when the truth would help them? Most of us have, consciously or unconsciously. Evil talk comes easily to all of us. Are you able to walk away from evil talk and not participate in it? Are you able to stand up to it?

May my words always be words that you would be proud of, my God.

For more: See James 4:11—evil talk is a problem everywhere.

THOMAS MORE
(1478–1535)

Oh, the joys of those who . . . delight in the law of Yahweh, and ponder it day and night. (Psalm 1:1–2)

"I die the king's good servant, but God's first." These are the last words uttered by Thomas More, scholar, chancellor of England, and a holy man. He was beheaded by the order of King Henry VIII. Thomas More's dying words remind us of our own priorities. In the end we owe allegiance to God above all else. How often have we gone against our convictions? Would we be willing to die for our beliefs?

"Lord, grant me a heart that knows nothing of boredom, of weeping, and of sighing. Let me not be overly concerned with the bothersome thing I call 'myself.' Give me a sense of humor, and I will find happiness in life and profit for others." (Thomas More)

Put on the whole armor of God, so that you may be able to stand against the wiles of the devil. (Ephesians 6:11)

What exactly is the "armor of God"? The armor of God is praying in solitude, reading the words of God in the Scriptures, praying with a friend, serving others with charity, being hopeful. Do you have on your armor? Does it have any holes?

I want to surround myself with your armor, powerful and merciful God. Grant me faith, hope, and love—the armor that I need.

For more: Read Colossians 3:12–17, which uses a similar image, talking about clothes instead of armor.

June 24

Your word is a lamp for my steps, and a light to my path. (Psalm 119:105)

Think of how comforting a streetlight or a lighted footpath is on a dark night. Have you ever thought of God's word that way? Find some words from the Bible to be your special light.

God, your word is a lamp to my feet and a light to my path. Let me always walk in your light, especially when it seems that I am surrounded by darkness.

Can a woman forget her nursing child, or show no compassion for the child of her womb? Even these may forget, yet I will not forget you. (Isaiah 49:15)

Few bonds are as strong as those connecting a mother and her nursing child. The writer uses this image to convey how close we humans are to God. Yet even if a mother forgets her child, we are assured that God will never forget us. Think about that: We are—each of us—embraced forever by a loving God.

God, you are our father and our mother. You give us life and nourish us each day. May we never forget you, for we know you will never forget us.

June 26

Just like the clay in the potter's hand, so are you in my hand. (Jeremiah 18:6)

You may have worked with clay, and maybe even thrown a pot yourself or watched a potter in action. Imagine that God is the potter and you are the clay being carefully molded with God's loving hands. Unlike clay, though, we can refuse to be molded. How open are you to being shaped by the Master Potter?

God, you are the one who formed us within our mother's womb, and you continue to shape us. We know that each of us is being lovingly formed into something unique. May we be willing clay in your hands.

You are my help, and in the shadow of your wings I shout for joy. (Psalm 63:7)

Imagine yourself protected by a powerful eagle, safe in the shadow of the eagle's majestic wings. Or think of the places you could go on the eagle's wings and the things you would see. All you have to do is hold on and trust. God is your help and strength. Pray for God's protection and a soaring spirit.

God, you are my help. Increase my trust in you so that I can shout for joy, knowing that I am secure in the shadow of your wings and lifted up on the power of your wings.

June 28

Hatred stirs up strife, but love covers all offenses. (Proverbs 10:12)

A simple proverb, but one with much wisdom. Carrying hatred within us only causes us strife, as well as causing strife to the person who is the target of our hate. Love, on the other hand, can change lives. Do you have some pocket of hate in your heart? Can you turn that hatred to love, or at least to forgiveness?

God, fill my heart with love so that I can let go of the baggage of hatred that weighs me down and depresses my soul. Let me respond with love to those who have offended me.

APOSTLES PETER AND PAUL

And I tell you, you are Peter, and on this rock I will build my church. (Matthew 16:18)

The two cornerstones of the early church are certainly Peter and Paul. Between them they are responsible for giving shape and depth to the early Christian community. Peter was one of the twelve Apostles; Paul was converted to Christianity after Jesus' death. Both men suffered martyrdom in Rome. How can you be a rock of hope and strength to other people?

Dear God, thank you for these two great pillars of the early church. They were clearly human and frail, but both had deep faith in you. Help me to be a rock of faith that can serve and inspire others.

June 30

The Lord God took the man and put him in the garden of Eden to till it and keep it. (Genesis 2:15)

This passage from the second creation story reminds us that we humans are placed on this earth to care for it and keep it. American Indians made caring for the earth an important part of their spirituality. Christians are called to do the same. How do we show respect for our planet? How well do we take care of this garden Earth?

God, from the beginning you have placed us on Earth to take care of the earth and nurture it. Help us to be good gardeners and to treat all creation, especially the earth, with great respect.

I will bless Yahweh at all times; praise shall continually be in my mouth. (Psalm 34:1)

How can I live out this psalm verse today? How can I remind myself that I need to bless and praise God whenever possible? Here are a couple of ideas. Bless God by forming good habits of behavior, by doing small acts of kindness; each act blesses God. When you walk into a room, silently say to God, "Thanks, God." Doing these small blessings creates a habit that will stay with you "continually."

Good and gracious God, there is so much to praise you for. Remind me often today of your presence. Let words of blessing and praise come out of my mouth, rather than words that are harsh or negative.

July 2

I have learned to be content with whatever I have. (Philippians 4:11)

Every year our Jewish sisters and brothers celebrate Passover. This feast remembers when God freed the Jewish people from slavery in Egypt and led them to the Promised Land. As part of the Passover meal, the family offers thanksgiving for God's incredible generosity. One song, *"Dayyeinu,"* lists the many wonderful deeds God has done, ending each time with *dayyeinu,* meaning "it would have been enough." It would have been enough to be led out of Egypt. It would have been enough for you to give us food only once. The song goes on, listing all the things God did to free the Jewish people. While offering thanksgiving, the prayer also says that the Jewish people would have been content in whatever state God decided to put them in. Can we say the same thing?

I am grateful for all that you give me, God, and will be content wherever you lead me.

For more: Read the full story of the Exodus, found in the Book of Exodus.

I can do all things through him who strengthens me. (Philippians 4:13)

"I can do all things by myself"—well, not exactly, although we like to think it's true. We can do all things through God because God strengthens us. When we rely on our own strength and energy, we can get certain things done, but we cannot endure the difficult trials of life on our own. Only with God can we do and survive all things. We just need to trust and turn to God.

Help me to turn to you and depend on you, God, rather than myself alone. We can do great things together!

For more: Take a look at Psalm 91—we can endure all things within God's embrace.

U.S. INDEPENDENCE DAY

Go therefore and make disciples of all nations. (Matthew 28:19)

With the preceding words, a new religion was founded. Jesus told his disciples to spread the news about what God had done through him. Our life and the lives of millions would not be the same without these words. Today Americans celebrate the birth of the United States, a nation that has traditionally allowed people to practice religion freely. What does it mean to be openly Christian? Does freedom of religious expression make any difference in the way you live?

God, thank you for the ideal of religious freedom. May I use this right to openly spread the Good News through my words and my way of living.

For more: The story of the Exodus is Israel's independence movement. Read about the Exodus, especially beginning at chapter 7.

Show yourself in all respects a model of good works. (Titus 2:7)

People tend to watch those who claim to be Christians. Skeptics like to check their actions to see if those "Christians" really act like Christians. How does a disciple of Jesus act? If we say we are followers of Jesus, are we living as good models of charity, hope, and faith? What would people say about your Christian life at the end of the day?

May my life reflect my love for you, my God, and your love for me.

For more: Take a look at Psalm 1.

July 6

I am saying this so that no one may deceive you with plausible arguments. (Colossians 2:4)

One of the easiest ways we are tempted to evil is through things that sound great. This is especially true when we are told only pieces, often untrue, of the story. For example, we are told that sex only exists for our personal pleasure. We are not often reminded of the consequences of sex outside of a loving, committed relationship. Be careful when you hear about something that sounds too good to be true. It likely is, in fact, too good to be true.

God, give me wisdom, that I may not be led astray. Give me wisdom beyond my years.

Set your minds on things that are above, not on things that are on earth. (Colossians 3:2)

The expression "you can't take it with you" is an obvious reference to our desire to acquire things. We all want things, and we tend to turn those wants into needs: another phone line for our bedroom, a better stereo, the latest video game, new clothes—our list goes on and on. It's hard to focus on "things that are above" when we are preoccupied with "things that are on earth." Take a look around today at your things. Can you find ways to refocus on the things of God, the things that are good for your soul?

Help me to see my things on earth in perspective, O God.

For more: Reread the story of the prodigal son (Luke 15:11–32), and see how the younger son's focus on passing things got him into trouble.

July 8

But we have this treasure in clay jars, so that it may be made clear that this extraordinary power belongs to God and does not come from us. (2 Corinthians 4:7)

We have this treasure of ourselves in clay jars. During the time of Jesus, clay jars were used for storage, but they were fragile and easily broken. This verse compares us to fragile clay jars. Does this mean that we are weak and fragile? Not necessarily. On our own we are, but we have the power of God in us, and it is God's power, not our own, that makes us strong. Has there been a time in your life when you felt fragile, but the power of God within you made you strong?

Thank you, God, for always supporting this clay jar: me. I especially need your power in this (name the situation). Be with me, God of power.

For more: Read all of Second Corinthians, chapter 4.

When I look at your heavens, the work of your hands, the moon and stars which you have created—who are we that you should be mindful of us, that you should care for us? (Psalm 8:3–4)

Spend some time one of these summer evenings gazing at the night sky. The universe is so vast that we can easily feel that we are insignificant. But we're not! We are an important part of God's creation. Keep that in mind as you look at the moon or try to count the stars.

God, thank you for the awesome beauty of nature, especially the night sky. The stars are so far away and so numerous, and yet you know each of them—and us—by name. You care for us. Let us never take that for granted.

July 10

Sing psalms, hymns, and spiritual songs to God. (Colossians 3:16)

Singing is praying twice. This is old wisdom rooted in the Bible. One great way to praise God is with music. It is a gift of God, and it is a way for us to give praise. Is there a way you could incorporate the music you enjoy into your faith life, in order that you may give praise? Maybe take a song that means a lot to you and use it as a prayer tonight before you turn off the lights. Try it!

I know there are many ways to praise you, God. Thank you for all of them, but especially for music.

For more: When the Israelites entered the Promised Land, Miriam led them in praise of God by song and dance (Exodus, chapter 15).

BENEDICT
(CA. 480–547)

Now the whole group of those who believed were of one heart and soul, and no one claimed private ownership of any possessions, but everything they owned was held in common. (Acts of the Apostles 4:32)

This description of the early Christians is the ideal that Benedict strove for when he set about founding monastic communities. *Monk* comes from the word *mono,* meaning "one." A monk was to focus on one goal: loving God. Today the spirit of Benedict, with its stress on community, prayer, and hospitality, lives on in the many Benedictine monasteries throughout the world. What would it be like to live the kind of life described in the above passage from Acts?

O God, help me to seek greater communion with you and with other people. May I remember Benedict's words, "Let us open our eyes to the light that comes from God, and our ears to the voice from heaven that every day calls out."

July 12

Whatever your task, put yourselves into it as done for the Lord and not for your masters, since you know that from the Lord you will receive the inheritance as your reward; you serve the Lord Christ. (Colossians 3:23–24)

It is much easier to do service work when we are doing work that we enjoy or when our work is being recognized. But what about when we are given a task that we dislike, or when our important task goes unnoticed? The next time you feel as if your good works are being ignored or shortchanged, try to remember this text and be aware that you are serving God. You might gain another perspective on your work.

God, if I work well, with good intention and motivated by a desire to serve people, I know that I am serving you too, even when my work seems insignificant or ignored. Guide me, my Creator.

For more: Read the parable of the rich man and Lazarus in Luke 16:19–31. Lazarus is finally noticed in heaven.

Arise, Yahweh! O God, lift up your hand! Forget not the afflicted. (Psalm 10:12)

God never forgets the afflicted, but we might. Look around your school, neighborhood, workplace, and family. Watch the news or read the front page of a newspaper. Who is being afflicted, oppressed, held down? What can you do to help? How best can you do God's work?

O God, overlooking those who are afflicted is easy; forgetting about them is even easier, especially if things are going well for me. Open my eyes and my heart so that I may help afflicted people as I can.

July 14

Give my greetings . . . to Nympha and the church in her house. (Colossians 4:15)

The early church was not a church as we know it today. In fact the early churches were actually small groups of people who met in members' houses—in this case in Nympha's house. Where we spend our time is significant, for it tells a lot about us. Where do you spend your time? Where would someone send greetings to you through someone else? What would they know about you from this place?

God of compassion, may I realize that you are always with me, and may I make wherever I am, a place of welcome for you.

For more: Read about the building of the first Temple in First Kings, chapter 6.

My child, . . . keep my commandments and live, keep my teachings as the apple of your eye. (Proverbs 7:1–2)

Good advice. We know the teachings of Jesus, and we have heard the commandments. What prevents us from keeping them? Ask for God's help in keeping whatever commandment is hardest for you.

God, I am your child, and I stray from you easily. Help me to stay on the right path, the one that leads to you. Help me to keep your teachings as the "apple of [my] eye."

July 16

For surely I know the plans I have for you, says the LORD, *plans for your welfare and not for harm, to give you a future with hope. (Jeremiah 29:11)*

Jeremiah gave this message of hope to a group of people who had been taken away from their homes and forced into slavery. Babylon was a bad place for the Jews, but God, through Jeremiah, asked them to be patient and to trust. Sometimes in our life, we have it bad too. Ask today for the gifts of patience and trust in God's care.

God, thank you for being trustworthy. It amazes me that you are able to care for me, among all your people. Help me to learn patience and trust so that I will be able to find the future with hope that you have planned for me.

For more: Check out Isaiah, chapter 43, to see how much God loves you and has great hopes for you.

Let us hold fast to the confession of our hope without wavering, for he who has promised is faithful. (Hebrews 10:23)

Hope is important to Christians. Jesus is hope. Because he cared enough to die for our sins, we can be forgiven if we only remain faithful ourselves. List three hopes you have for your life, and put them in a safe place where you can review them another day.

Dear God, you know my secret hopes and how important they are to me. I pray that you would confirm the hopes that lead me closer to you and deny the hopes that bring me to harm.

For more: Read Hebrews 10:19–39, and hear what it means to hold fast to our confession of hope.

July 18

Moses' father-in-law [Jethro] said to him, "What you are doing is not good." (Exodus 18:17)

From ancient times families have been keeping family members in line. Jethro was concerned that Moses was doing too much, and Moses was wise enough to listen to him. Can you think of a time when a family member's advice helped you make a good decision?

Dear God, thank you for my family and for the ways they show their love for me. Help me to be open to their suggestions, even when they come unasked for.

For more: Sharing responsibilities is always a good idea. Read First Corinthians, chapter 12, to see how we are expected to work together as one Body in Christ.

Amazement seized all of them, and they glorified God and were filled with awe, saying, "We have seen strange things today." (Luke 5:26)

Sometimes a miracle is just so big that all we can do is stand back in amazement. That's what happened when Jesus cured the paralyzed man in this story from Luke. Jesus cured the man partly because of the love of the friends who lowered the man through the roof of a crowded house where Jesus was speaking. Bring the touch of Christ to one of your friends today by forgiving or by just listening.

Dear God, bringing your touch to the world is a big responsibility. Sometimes it feels fine, but at other times I'm not sure that I'm equal to it. Help me to know what to say and how to act so that my life reflects your presence in my heart.

For more: Take time to read this story in Luke 5:17–26, and imagine that you are the paralyzed person on the stretcher.

July 20

Do not withhold good from those to whom it is due, when it is in your power to do it. (Proverbs 3:27)

All through the Scriptures, we hear about sharing, being generous, making allowances for those who are less fortunate than we are. Sometimes the best good we can do is to share a smile or a simple greeting. Today make it a point to greet persons you meet with a smile. If you know their name, be sure to greet each one by name.

Dear God, thank you for the little things, like smiles, that you have given freely to all of us to share with one another. Thank you for all the people who have brought good into my life; help me to be someone who passes it on.

For more: Look in Matthew, chapter 5, to hear one sermon that Jesus gave about sharing ourselves with others.

For where there is envy and selfish ambition, there will also be disorder and wickedness of every kind. (James 3:16)

Envy creeps into our heart so easily! Construction takes so much more effort than destruction. Yet we are warned against envy and selfishness because they bring destruction. Examine your heart for envy today, and if you find any, offer it to God. Make a list of all your gifts, talents, skills, abilities; build those up and thank God for them.

Dear God, I pray that envy might never take up permanent residence in my heart. Help me to celebrate from my heart the success of other people, and give me the insight to learn from my own failures.

For more: Read James 3:13–18 to find out what virtues counteract envy and selfish ambition.

MARY MAGDALENE

Mary Magdalene went and announced to the disciples, "I have seen the Lord." (John 20:18)

Jesus found a good friend and devoted follower in Mary Magdalene. She had dealt with many difficulties in her life, and she chose to follow Jesus in spite of them all. In fact she was one of the first people to whom he appeared after he rose from the dead. Ask God to give you a friend as faithful to you as Mary Magdalene was to Jesus.

Dear God, thank you for my friends, especially for the ones who I know would stand by me no matter what the situation. Thank you, Holy Friend, for being so forgiving and loving. I know you are my friend even when I've done some really stupid things.

For more: Check out John 20:1–18 to hear how Mary encountered Jesus at the tomb on Easter.

When a man makes a vow to the LORD, or swears an oath to bind himself by a pledge, he shall not break his word; he shall do according to all that proceeds out of his mouth. (Numbers 30:2)

In the days before written contracts and lawyers, when people gave their word on a business deal or on an agreement of any kind, it meant that they would follow through. Does your word carry that same commitment? Take time to consider your words before you speak today.

Faithful God, if I had to follow through on everything I ever said, I would be busy for the rest of my life. Help me to remember that my words go further than I realize, and that I need to consider them before they escape my mouth.

For more: Find James, chapter 5, and read how, even after Jesus died and rose, the power of a person's word was still important.

July 24

But as for you . . . pursue righteousness, godliness, faith, love, endurance, gentleness. (1 Timothy 6:11)

When we work toward righteousness, godliness, faith, love, endurance, and gentleness, we keep ourselves busy growing in Christ, instead of being distracted by other pursuits. Write this verse on a small card and put it where it can serve as a reminder.

Dear God, I praise and thank you for the grace you give to help me find my way to you. Please guide my footsteps every day so that I become righteous, godly, faithful, loving, patient, and gentle.

For more: Although Paul refers to Timothy as "young," he makes it clear that Timothy has an important role in the church. Read First Timothy, and imagine that Paul is writing to you.

THE APOSTLE JAMES

As [Jesus] went a little farther, he saw James son of Zebedee and his brother John, who were in their boat mending the nets. Immediately he called them; and they left their father Zebedee in the boat with the hired men, and followed him. (Mark 1:19–20)

James and his brother, John, left everything behind to follow Jesus. What was it about Jesus that made his invitation so compelling? How much are you willing to leave behind to follow Christ?

Holy One, you call each of us as you did James and John. So often, though, our life is so cluttered with noise and distractions that we do not heed your call. Help me to follow you with an open and willing heart.

JOACHIM AND ANN

Let us now sing the praises of famous men [and women], our ancestors in their generations. . . . Their wealth will remain with their descendants, and their inheritance with their children's children. (Sirach 44:1,11)

Though no specific reference is made in the Bible to Mary's parents, Ann and Joachim, this day has been set aside to celebrate these two special people. The many legends about Ann and Joachim serve to remind us that Jesus had grandparents who cared about him, just as we do. Take a moment to reflect on the special gift that grandparents are in your life.

Dear God, thank you for your Son, Jesus; for his parents, Mary and Joseph; and also for his grandparents. Thank you also for the special role that grandparents play in our life. Bless all grandparents today.

Then Jesus said to him, "Put your sword back into its place; for all who take the sword will perish by the sword." (Matthew 26:52)

We don't fight much with swords anymore, but we do disagree with one another—sometimes with siblings, parents, and friends. Do you say things intended to hurt? Do you tell nasty stories to turn people against the one you are mad at? Do you hold grudges? The way we fight will also be used against us someday. Are you comfortable with that?

God, help me always to disagree and argue fairly with others in our conflicts. May I realize that winning is not the only thing. Good relationships are much more important.

For more: See how Sarah dealt with Hagar in their disagreement (Genesis, chapter 16).

The reason I speak to them in parables is that "seeing they do not perceive, and hearing they do not listen, nor do they understand." (Matthew 13:13)

Oftentimes we do not hear the real truth in stories, either in the stories that Jesus tells, that our friends tell, or that we tell. The next time someone tells you a story, listen very carefully. What are they really telling you about themselves? What are the stories that are important to you? What do they tell others about you?

God, help me to be a better listener, to hear what others are really telling me.

For more: Read the passage about Nathan telling David a story (Second Samuel, chapters 11 and 12). He is really telling David the story of his life.

MARTHA

The Lord answered her, "Martha, Martha, you are worried and distracted by many things; there is need of only one thing. Mary has chosen the better part, which will not be taken away from her." (Luke 10:41–42)

Poor Martha. She was so preoccupied with cleaning and cooking and running around that Jesus has to remind her that sometimes those tasks can be set aside for a greater good. Her sister, Mary, was seated at Jesus' feet. Sometimes we need to just sit in the presence of God and not worry about the many things that need to get done.

Living God, help me to never get so caught up in the many tasks I have to accomplish each day that I forget to spend time with you. Slow me down, and let me sit quietly at your feet and listen to what you have to say to me.

July 30

Do not give what is holy to dogs. (Matthew 7:6)

Jesus is not antidog here. He is raising a lot of questions for us: What is holy or sacred in our life? Is our family sacred? Do we recognize the support and love they give us, or do we throw them to the dogs by making fun of them with our friends, by being embarrassed to be seen with them?

I want to honor and respect my family, God. Help me to love better.

For more: Turn to Exodus, chapter 20, and reread the Commandments. What does it mean to honor your father and your mother?

IGNATIUS OF LOYOLA (1491–1556)

Sing Yahweh a new song! . . . Tell God's glory among the nations; tell God's wondrous deeds to all people. (Psalm 96:1–3)

As a young soldier of fortune, Ignatius was badly wounded in battle in his native Spain. During his recovery he read books about Christ and about the lives of the saints. He soon dedicated his life to God's service, and went on to found the Jesuits, one of the largest and most famous religious societies in the Catholic church. He urged his followers to live out this saying: "All for the greater glory of God."

"Take, Lord, and receive all my liberty, my memory, my understanding, and my whole will. You have given me all that I have, all that I am, and I surrender all to your divine will, that you dispose of me. Give me only your love and your grace. With this I am rich enough, and I have no more to ask." (Ignatius)

August 1

And you became imitators of us and of the Lord. (1 Thessalonians 1:6)

We all have people we look up to. Oftentimes these people serve as models for us, and consciously or unconsciously, we strive to imitate them. Who are the people you look up to? What aspects of their lives do you strive to imitate? Do you think someone will want to imitate you someday?

Jesus, I want to imitate your love for God and for others.

For more: Read about the friendship between David and Jonathan (First Samuel, chapter 20).

You turned to God from idols, to serve a living and true God. (1 Thessalonians 1:9)

What does it mean to serve a living God? Maybe a better question is, What does it mean to be alive? We have this life force—a soul—that can direct us to living fully. We can experience joy and pain, happiness and sadness, and we can decide what we want to do and not do. Our God is alive, standing with us in tough times, feeling our pain and our joy, calling us to the good life.

Holy Companion, I want to serve you with all my soul and in all my actions. May I always know that you are with me.

For more: Read the story of the Tower of Babel, and see God making decisions (Genesis 11:1–9).

August 3

But we were gentle among you, like a nurse tenderly caring for her own children. (1 Thessalonians 2:7)

This passage was written from one Christian community to the church in Thessalonica, but it is a wonderful image for God as well. God actively cares for us, like a nurse taking care of her children. Like a nurse when we are sick or hurting, God stays up with us, making sure we have what we need. God tucks us in when we feel alone and miserable. When is the last time you felt like you were nursed by God? If you don't feel this way, maybe you need to call on God. Prayer is the call button.

God, thank you for the amazing way you love and care for me.

For more: Another wonderful image for God is that of the mother eagle pushing her young out of the nest so they will learn to fly. See Isaiah 40:31 or Deuteronomy 32:11.

For God did not call us to impurity, but in holiness. (1 Thessalonians 4:7)

People tend to think that to be holy means to be perfect. Well, not really. To be holy is to live to serve God and our neighbor the best that we can with our talents and gifts. Some people, such as Dorothy Day or Mother Teresa, are able to do that in extraordinary ways. But thousands of others live quiet, holy lives right under our nose. Do you know any holy people? Who are they?

God, bless the quiet, holy people who do the right thing without recognition. Lead me to be one of them eventually. In the meantime help me to do the best I can.

For more: Mary led a life of holiness, not because she gave birth to Jesus but because she said "Yes!" to God. Read about it in the first chapter of Luke. See also Leviticus 11:44.

August 5

Therefore encourage one another and build up each other. (1 Thessalonians 5:11)

How often do you say something nice to someone just because you feel like it? Take some time today to notice the people around you and give them some positive feedback or thanks. Sometimes a kind comment can change someone's day.

God of goodness, without being too innocent, may I still see the good in others and help them to know that they are good.

For more: Read about the reconciliation of Jacob and Esau, two brothers who were estranged (Genesis 33:1–11). After reconciling they build up each other.

TRANSFIGURATION

Jesus took with him Peter and James and his brother John and led them up a high mountain, by themselves. And he was transfigured before them, and his face shone like the sun, and his clothes became dazzling white. (Matthew 17:1–2)

What an amazing scene this must have been! Today we celebrate this remarkable vision that Jesus shared with three of his followers. It gave them a glimpse of the dazzling glory that was part of the divine nature of Jesus. Try to imagine what this must have been like.

Holy One, I praise you for the mystery of your divinity and your humanity. Your Transfiguration reminds us that there is so much glory in you that most people you encountered simply could not imagine it. But I know that you are indeed the Son of God, and I praise you.

For more: Read two more Gospel accounts of the Transfiguration in chapter 9 of both Mark and Luke.

August 7

I have chosen the way of [faithfulness]. (Psalm 119:30)

Is this statement one we can live up to? The way of faithfulness is not an easy one, but it is filled with rewards. Faithfulness is often, to quote the poet Robert Frost, "the road less traveled by." What small thing can you do today to choose the way of faithfulness?

O God, we need to choose the way of faithfulness, the way that leads to you, each day. Let me take the steps necessary to make sure I am on the way to you today.

DOMINIC
(1170–1221)

How beautiful upon the mountains are the feet of the messenger who announces peace, who brings good news, who announces salvation. (Isaiah 52:7)

Dominic founded a religious community called the Order of Preachers, more commonly known as the Dominicans. Dominic believed that effective preaching is essential to spreading the Gospel, and he insisted that his followers be well trained in the Scriptures and in theology. The early Dominicans were told that if they were to be preachers of the Good News, they had to be "earnest . . . in their study, always reading or thinking, . . . and striving to retain as much as they can." How can your study be done for the glory of God?

Dear God, help me to be, like Dominic, a bearer of good news. Help me to heed well the message I hear preached and taught to me, for I believe that you are speaking through your preachers and teachers.

NAGASAKI MEMORIAL DAY

Blessed are the peacemakers, for they will be called children of God. (Matthew 5:9)

On this day in 1945, the second atomic bomb was dropped on Japan by the United States. The first was dropped three days earlier on Hiroshima. Today is a good time to pause and reflect on the nightmare of war and the importance of being a peacemaker. Peace begins in each of our hearts. How can you serve as a peacemaker today?

God of peace, forgive us the horrors we inflict on one another in times of war. Give me the determination to avoid violence and to strive to settle my differences peacefully. Help me to be a peacemaker.

LAWRENCE

Each of you must give as you have made up your mind, not reluctantly or under compulsion, for God loves a cheerful giver. (2 Corinthians 9:7)

Lawrence is an early martyr with a sense of humor. When Roman officials demanded that he turn over the treasures of the church, he brought forth the blind, the lame, and the needy. He was ordered to be roasted to death over a fire, and according to legend, he is said to have joked: "Turn me over. I'm done on this side." How can a sense of humor help us cope with difficult situations?

Living God, thank you for the reminder from the life and death of Lawrence that a sense of humor is truly a gift to a world that is often too serious and grim. Help me to be a cheerful giver and not to count the cost. May I bring a smile and service to someone who needs them today.

August 11

See that none of you repays evil for evil, but always seek to do good to one another and to all. (1 Thessalonians 5:15)

It doesn't seem fair. If someone does something really awful to us, we should be able to do something just as mean back to them. After all, they asked for it, right? This is one of the greatest challenges of being a disciple of Jesus. We become better people, more Christlike, when we are good to all, especially when what we really want to do is repay evil with evil. Repaying evil with good multiplies good; we all gain. Repaying with evil multiplies evil; then we all suffer.

Help me to do good to all and to resist the temptation to hurt those who have hurt me.

For more: Rachel (Genesis 29:9–30) was dealt with unfairly. See how she responded.

Health and fitness are better than any gold, and a robust body than countless riches. (Sirach 30:15)

This could be the motto of any health club or gym. The words sound contemporary. The simple truth is that they are as relevant today as they were when they were written some twenty-five hundred years ago. What are you doing to stay fit and healthy?

O God, help me to stay fit and to make healthy choices. That way I can serve you better. You need robust workers to spread your word and your love. Let me value my health and strive to stay as fit as I am able.

August 13

Give thanks in all circumstances. (1 Thessalonians 5:18)

Someone once went to a friend to ask for advice because she was having trouble forgiving someone who had hurt her. Her friend asked if she had thanked God for the experience. "Why would I thank God for so much hurt and pain?" she asked. The friend asked if she had learned anything. Of course she had. The wise friend told her that it is only when we are able to thank God for the experience that we will be able to forgive. We shouldn't give thanks just for the good experiences, but rather "give thanks in all circumstances."

May I always be able to find the good in every situation, O God.

For more: Read the story of Abraham and Isaac (Genesis, chapter 22), and then reread it as if you were Isaac. What did Isaac learn? Also reread Matthew 5:21–26.

MAXIMILIAN KOLBE

No one has greater love than this, to lay down one's life for one's friends. (John 15:13)

These words from John's Gospel were quoted by Pope John Paul II when he declared Maximilian Kolbe to be a saint. This Franciscan priest stepped forward to take the place of a family man who was to be killed along with nine other men as punishment for the escape of a prisoner from Auschwitz, one of the Nazi death camps. The ten men were starved to death, and through it all, Maximilian Kolbe led his companions in prayer and prepared them for death. Kolbe once said, "When the occasion presents itself to call the attention of society . . . to some evil, it must be done with love for the person to blame."

Merciful God, there are many such stories of heroism and courage that have emerged from the horrors of the Nazi concentration camps. We praise you for the courage of people such as Anne Frank, Elie Wiesel, Viktor Frankl, Oscar Schindler, and especially today Maximilian Kolbe, who gave his life so another might live.

THE ASSUMPTION OF MARY INTO HEAVEN

A great portent appeared in heaven: a woman clothed with the sun, with the moon under her feet, and on her head a crown of twelve stars. (Revelation 12:1)

Christians have long believed that after Mary's death, God raised her body to heaven, and she lives with God forever. Today we celebrate this as a holy day to remind ourselves of Mary's special role in the story of our salvation.

Hail Mary, full of grace, the Lord is with you. Blessed are you among women, and blessed is the fruit of your womb, Jesus. Holy Mary, mother of God, pray for us sinners, now and at the hour of our death.

Now we command you, beloved, in the name of our Lord Jesus Christ, to keep away from believers who are living in idleness. (2 Thessalonians 3:6)

An old expression talks about idleness being the devil's workshop. Though that may be a bit exaggerated, it is much easier to be led away from God when we are not focused. Do you find yourself with a lot of free time? Do you have any ideas for filling it with service to others and to God?

May I always use my time wisely, God, and may I serve you in all that I do.

For more: Jonah found himself with lots of free time that he eventually used to serve God. Read about it in the Book of Jonah.

August 17

The aim of such instruction is love that comes from a pure heart, a good conscience, and sincere faith. (1 Timothy 1:5)

Sometimes our own needs keep us from loving from a pure heart. Who are the people you love? Why do you love them? Your answer to the second question will tell you volumes about your own heart. Do you love people because of what they do for you, or do you love them for who they are?

God, I want to love people for who they are, not because they make me feel good.

For more: Chapter 13 of the First Letter to the Corinthians tells about love from a pure heart. See what it has to say.

Jealousy and anger shorten life, and anxiety brings on premature old age. (Sirach 30:24)

This is all about stress. What are the things that often stress you out: jealousy and anger? worrying that doesn't do you any good? It's good to know that even the writer of Sirach knew that stress is not good for us. What are you anxious about today? Why?

O God, help me to dump the things that are weighing me down and stressing me out, especially jealousy, anger, and anxiety. Let me take a deep breath when I find myself feeling stressed, and find my peace in you.

August 19

By rejecting conscience, certain persons have suffered shipwreck in the faith. (1 Timothy 1:19)

Christianity gives us some guidelines and "do's and don'ts" for how we should live our life. But this passage is clear: simply following those rules is not enough. We need to be led by our conscience. Does that mean we ignore the church's guidance? No. But we do need to understand the reason for the teachings so that we can follow the guidelines in good conscience, not just blindly. Is there something the church teaches that you don't understand? See if you can find out why the church teaches what it teaches.

God, I want to follow your guidelines for my life in good conscience—not just follow blindly!

For more: See Romans, chapter 3, on the relationship between the Law and faith.

I slept, but my heart was awake. Listen! my beloved is knocking. (Song of Solomon 5:2)

The Song of Solomon catches the passion of someone in love. We have all dreamed on occasion of a special love. God loves us so much that each of us is "the one" for God. Imagine that God expressed this intimate love to you. Could you respond back in love?

God who is love, when I look at creation, my friends, my family, and my life, I can see that you really do love me. Please help me to express my love for you through my appreciation of these expressions of your divine love.

For more: Find Deuteronomy 6:4–8 in the Hebrew Scriptures. Even in our earliest roots, we find God asking for our love.

August 21

I tell you, on the day of judgment you will have to give an account for every careless word you utter; for by your words you will be justified, and by your words you will be condemned. (Matthew 12:36–37)

Quotes like this from Jesus' public ministry can really frighten us. Imagine every careless word you have ever uttered returning to you on the judgment day! Today decide to count to five before you answer anyone who speaks to you, so that you can consider your replies.

Dear God, I am grateful for the gift of speech and the world of communication that this gift opens for me. Please forgive me for the times when I have used this gift carelessly or selfishly, and help me to have a fresh start today.

For more: Read Matthew 12:32–37 to hear what Jesus had to say about the power of words.

All spoke well of him and were amazed at the gracious words that came from his mouth. They said, "Is not this Joseph's son?" (Luke 4:22)

As we mature and come to an understanding of life, sometimes those around us are unable to accept our growth. When we become the people God created us to be, we amaze others, just like Jesus amazed those around him. Will you dare to be true to the person you know God created you to be?

Dear God, I grow more and more each day, but those around me don't always seem to notice. I feel that I am constantly seen as and treated like a kid. Please help me hang in there with my new maturity so that I can continue to grow in you.

For more: Jesus did go back to his hometown. Read Luke 4:14–30 to see what happened to him.

August 23

You love true sincerity, so you teach me the depths of wisdom. (Psalm 51:6)

We can fool a lot of the people a lot of the time. God asks us to be honest, even when we are able to fool almost everybody. The truth is that in the end, we only have to live with ourselves. Are you honest with yourself about yourself?

Holy God, there are things about me that I don't like. I try to hide them, even from you. Please teach me wisdom in my secret heart so that I can learn to face my fears and other feelings instead of trying to hide them.

For more: Psalm 51 is the psalm of David to God after David had fooled himself into thinking that God would not notice that he had stolen someone else's wife.

You are my sheep, the sheep of my pasture, and I am your God, says the Lord GOD. (Ezekiel 34:31)

Sheep are fairly dumb and totally dependent. As the "sheep" of God's flock, our intelligence and independence pale in comparison with God's all-knowing and all-powerful reality. Are you willing to follow God's lead like sheep follow a shepherd? (Actually, sheep don't follow all that well either.)

Dear God, I'm not sure I like being called a sheep. Then again, it wouldn't be that bad if you would provide for me like shepherds do for their sheep. Help me to trust that you do provide my every need, even when I don't always understand your logic.

For more: Check out John 10:11–18 to see what Jesus had to say about God as our shepherd.

August 25

Do not be afraid, little flock, for it is your Father's good pleasure to give you the kingdom. (Luke 12:32)

Just when we may begin to feel insulted that we are referred to as dumb sheep, Jesus reminds us that we have been entrusted with the entire Kingdom of God. What an honor for us! Do you take your responsibility as a caretaker of the Kingdom of God seriously?

Holy Wisdom, why do you trust me with the Kingdom if I am as simple as a sheep? Thank you for your trust and confidence in me. Please inspire me to take my responsibility seriously, as one of the caretakers.

For more: Read Luke 6:20–31 to find out who else has been promised the Kingdom and how we're expected to act to keep it.

The fear of the LORD is life indeed; filled with it one rests secure and suffers no harm. (Proverbs 19:23)

It seems like being afraid of God would make us more stressed, but the fear of the Lord translates into awe. When we find God awesome, we reflect God's ways in our life, and we have nothing to be stressed about. Are you in awe of God?

Awesome God, thank you for creation, for making me, for paying attention to every single detail of my life. You are awesome!

For more: Find Psalm 107 and read about how awesome God is.

MONICA

Ask, and it will be given you; search, and you will find; knock, and the door will be opened for you. (Matthew 7:7)

Monica was the mother of Augustine of Hippo, a difficult young man who became a great theologian and bishop. He did everything he could to avoid God, but Monica never stopped praying for him. She once declared, "Nothing is far from God." This applied to Augustine too. Even though changing her son's heart looked hopeless, she had faith, and he did turn his life around. Is there someone or something you find hopeless? Start praying.

Dear God, thank you for great role models like Monica who hang in there with prayer. Help me to trust, like she did, that my prayers will have a positive effect if I am faithful to them.

For more: Read Luke 18:1–8 to hear a parable about a widow and a judge that speaks about hanging in there with your requests.

AUGUSTINE

God is love, and those who abide in love abide in God, and God abides in them. (1 John 4:16)

Augustine was a great teacher, and one of his famous teachings is, "Love, and do as you will." This is not as easy as it sounds. When we really, truly love everybody all the time, we can never do anything against the will of God, because God is love. Invite the Holy Spirit to bring God's love into your heart today.

God of love, thank you for the gift of love that you offer so freely to us all. Please send your Holy Spirit into my heart so that your love can live there and I can be truly free to do as I will.

For more: Read First Corinthians, chapter 13, to learn some of the qualities of Christian love.

August 29

You are my witnesses, says the Lord, *and my servant whom I have chosen, so that you may know and believe me and understand that I am he. Before me no god was formed, nor shall there be any after me. (Isaiah 43:10)*

We are so used to having religion around us that we forget there was a time when people had to be introduced to our God. Our understanding of the one God was revealed to many prophets so that we could know God the way we do today. Have you ever thanked God for caring enough to share divine understanding with us?

Dear God, in some ways I really do take you for granted because it seems like you've always been around. Thank you for giving us true knowledge of you through the prophets, the Scriptures, and our faith tradition.

For more: Read Ephesians 4:5–6 to hear the things Paul writes from prison about our one God.

We cannot keep from speaking about what we have seen and heard. (Acts of the Apostles 4:20)

When we actually meet God in our prayer, in our practice of faith, or in our life experiences, we just can't keep it in. It's like falling in love; we want everyone else to know the incredibly wonderful feelings we are experiencing, even though they are nearly impossible to communicate. Do you joyfully share your experiences of God with others?

God of wonder, I want to come to know you so well that I feel comfortable speaking about you to others. Please journey with me as I continue to find my life's path, so that I can joyfully share my experiences of you with others.

For more: Read Acts of the Apostles 3:1–4:22 to find out what was so amazing that the Apostles just had to speak about it.

August 31

Do not speak harshly to an older man, but speak to him as to a father. (1 Timothy 5:1)

Our elders have a lot of wisdom that we do not always acknowledge. Rather, we might tend to disregard old people as foolish. But Timothy tells us that we are to treat elders with respect and dignity. Who are the elders in your life? Have you learned from them? Could you learn more from them by asking? Take some time to sit down with your elders—you might find it fascinating!

Thank you for the wisdom you have given to my elders, God.

For more: Just before Moses died, he left "words of wisdom." See Deuteronomy, chapter 32.

God, you are my light and my salvation; whom shall I fear? (Psalm 27:1)

Fear can be crippling, especially when we are afraid of others. With God on our side, why are we so afraid? Who can really harm us?

God, remind us often that we should fear no one. You are our stronghold, our rock of safety in the storms of life. We have nothing to fear.

September 2

My child, when you come to serve the Lord, prepare yourselves for testing. (Sirach 2:1)

We know that to truly serve God means that we will be tested, because so much in life can lead us astray. Not only that, but God calls us to live life fully, using all our talents, our gifts, and our ability to love and care. Living fully tests us for sure. How have you been tested lately? What tests in life do you find the hardest to pass?

God, we have no right to expect that we will not be tested and tried as we resolve to serve you. Help us to be strong as we strive to serve you better.

God added his testimony by signs and wonders and various miracles, and by gifts of the Holy Spirit, distributed according to his will. (Hebrews 2:4)

We tend to think of miracles as dramatic events that happened only in biblical times. But God can be more subtle, and miracles can slip by us silently every day if we are not paying attention. Look around. Can you see God's "ordinary miracles" in the world today?

God, help me to be more aware of the miracles you work in my life.

For more: Read Matthew 6:26–34 about more "ordinary miracles."

ALBERT SCHWEITZER (1875–1965)

These good of heart lend graciously, handling their affairs honestly. Kept safe by virtue, they are always steadfast and leave an everlasting memory behind them. (Psalm 112:5–6)

Physician, musician, writer Albert Schweitzer gave up a comfortable and successful life in Europe to begin a medical practice among poor people in West Africa. He devoted his life to serving others, and was awarded the Nobel Peace Prize in 1958. He left us these words: "The only ones among you who will be truly happy are those who have sought and found a way to serve."

Divine Physician, your example at the Last Supper when you washed the feet of your Apostles was a powerful lesson in service. Albert Schweitzer lived out that example. Thank you for his lifelong witness of service to others. Inspire us to do the same.

MOTHER TERESA

The kingdom of heaven is like a mustard seed that someone took and sowed in his field; it is the smallest of all the seeds, but when it has grown it is the greatest of shrubs and becomes a tree. (Matthew 13:31–32)

Mother Teresa started her ministry by helping the homeless, dying people of Calcutta, India. In the end her efforts to help Christ, whom she saw daily in poor people, started a community that helps thousands of people worldwide. She said: "A joyful heart is the inevitable result of a heart burning with love. Never let anything so fill you with sorrow as to make you forget the joy of the Christ risen." Can you find some small way to help Christ in your everyday life?

God, lover of poor people, thank you for giving us great examples of people building your Reign, like Mother Teresa. Give me the confidence I need to follow through on my commitments, so that my small mustard-seed efforts can begin to grow.

For more: Keep reading in Matthew 13:44–48 to hear some other parables of the Kingdom of God.

September 6

Now when Jesus came into the district of Caesarea Philippi, he asked his disciples, "Who do people say that the Son of Man is?" (Matthew 16:13)

Even Jesus wondered what people were saying about him. He asked his disciples—who were his close friends—to tell him what they had heard. Sometimes it's good to check in with our friends to see how we are coming across to others. Ask a friend for some feedback about how you come across.

Holy Friend, knowing what my friends think of me is important, and I hope that I can learn more about myself by listening to what my friends have to say. Thank you for giving us one another to share our life stories with.

For more: Read the whole story of this question in Matthew 16:13–20. Who do you say that Jesus is to you?

O God, make haste to rescue me! Come to my aid! (Psalm 70:1)

All of us have times when we're in trouble. Whether we cause it ourselves or those around us seem to be out of control, we do need a helping hand. Don't forget that God wants to help, but only if we invite God into our life. Are you in trouble? Invite God to deliver you from it. Use the words of Psalm 70, "O God, come to my aid with (name the help you need)."

Help-filled God, thank you for standing by me in my times of trouble. Sometimes I forget that you have offered so many times to help. Please inspire me to call you in when the rest of the world walks out.

For more: Psalm 70 is a wonderful psalm for when we feel unjustly accused or wronged by others. Take some time to read the whole psalm.

September 8

But those who wait for the LORD shall renew their strength, they shall mount up with wings like eagles, they shall run and not be weary, they shall walk and not faint. (Isaiah 40:31)

When we have faith in God already and a crisis comes along, we are in the practice of turning to God. So we do. But if we wait until a crisis comes to establish connections to God, we might forget to ask for help. Resolve today to put aside some small amount of time each day to get to know God. Even a couple of minutes on the way to school or as you get up in the morning can make connections.

Ever-present God, you are easy to talk to. I am grateful that you continually reach out to have a relationship with me. Help me to get to know you better so that when a crisis comes along, I am prepared to turn to you.

For more: Go to Matthew 14:22–33 to see how Peter got into trouble, and how Jesus helped after Peter cried out, "Save me!"

Be alert at all times, praying that you may have the strength to escape all these things that will take place, and to stand before the Son of Man. (Luke 21:36)

We really don't know when the end of the world will happen. We don't even know when our own passing will come. Jesus challenges us to pray that we will be alert and ready every day. This is a great way to live anyway, because each moment is the only moment we really have. So if we live the moments well, we will live our life well. How are you doing this moment?

Eternal God, I get so busy thinking about the next hour, the next day, the next month, the next year that I forget about the only time I really have—right now. Let me enjoy the moment, pay attention to what I am doing right now, and in that way, make my life full. Then I won't have to worry about the end of the world or the end of this life.

For more: Read Luke, chapter 21, to see how Jesus describes the end of the world.

The eye that mocks a father and scorns to obey a mother will be pecked out by the ravens of the valley and eaten by the vultures. (Proverbs 30:17)

That's a pretty horrible image, isn't it! The fourth commandment tells us to honor our parents. We are reminded again here that our parents deserve our respect, even if we cannot agree with everything they say. Find some things about your parents to thank God for today.

Parent to us all, thank you for my parent(s). Help me to honor my parent(s), even if I have a difficult time loving them all the time.

For more: Read Ephesians, chapter 6, to learn about honoring our parents and those in authority over us.

Therefore prepare your minds for action; discipline yourselves; set all your hope on the grace that Jesus Christ will bring you when he is revealed. (1 Peter 1:13)

By now school has begun. Our minds are active. We pull ourselves together to do homework, get to class, and pay attention. We are challenged by Peter to set all our hope on the grace of Jesus Christ. Where have you set your hopes this year?

Holy Wisdom, my hopes are set on many things: good friends, relationships, grades, success. You can easily slip down to the bottom of my list. Help me to remember that when you come first, everything else will follow.

For more: Find Matthew 6:25–34 to learn about another teaching that puts Jesus and the Reign of God first.

September 12

I would rather take refuge in you, Yahweh, than rely on people. (Psalm 118:8)

It is really hard for us to know whom we can trust. Sometimes we trust our friends, and at other times our family. This psalm reminds us that the best place for our trust is always in God, because people change and move. We change and move, but God never changes. Where do you place your trust?

Faithful God, I pray that I can learn how to put more of my confidence in you. I want to believe that you will provide for my needs. When I put my trust in another person, remind me that you are here too. Thanks.

For more: God always loves us and waits for us to trust, even when we run away. Read Luke 15:11–32 to hear the parable of a young man who came to know his father's love and patience.

When they had prayed, the place in which they were gathered together was shaken; and they were all filled with the Holy Spirit and spoke the word of God with boldness. (Acts of the Apostles 4:31)

Even after Jesus sent the Holy Spirit upon the disciples the first time at Pentecost, they continued to pray for the Spirit to give them strength and courage. The Spirit brings the energy and life of Christ into our hearts. Ask the Holy Spirit to come into your heart today.

Dear God, thank you for the gift of the Holy Spirit, who brings our faith to life. Send the Spirit into my heart so that I may have the courage to truly live my faith in my everyday world.

For more: Read Acts of the Apostles, chapter 2, to learn more about the first outpouring of the Holy Spirit at Pentecost.

TRIUMPH OF THE CROSS

For the message about the cross is foolishness to those who are perishing, but to us who are being saved it is the power of God. (1 Corinthians 1:18)

The cross was an instrument of death, but it brought eternal life. Jesus rose, and when he did, he made it possible for every one of us to do the same when we die. Death cannot stop us because Jesus' sacrifice on the cross has won us salvation. Have you ever thanked Jesus for his sacrifice on your behalf?

God of mercy and compassion, thank you for sending your Son, Jesus, to die for us. Thank you for the gift of hope that springs from the great mystery of his death and Resurrection. Help me to remember that things are not always as they appear.

For more: Look in Luke 9:23–26 to see how we are challenged with regard to the cross.

But you, our God, are kind and true, patient, and ruling all things in mercy. (Wisdom of Solomon 15:1)

Mercy sounds old-fashioned, but we know when we need it. When we have messed up badly and gotten into deep trouble, what we need is mercy. We don't always get it from other humans, but God is always merciful. Do you have a place in your life where you could use God's patience and mercy right now? Ask!

Patient God, why is it so easy for me to notice everything that you ought to be fixing in everyone else and to miss the things that really need your fixing in me? Thank you for being patient with me as I continue to become my true self. Help me to show the same mercy to others that I expect from you.

For more: Check out Matthew 7:1–5 for a reminder on how we are to handle judging others.

September 16

So then, a Sabbath rest still remains for the people of God. (Hebrews 4:9)

The Scriptures place a lot of importance on rest. That's because rest is important for everyone. We all need a time for relaxation and rejuvenation, a time to refocus our energy, to re-create ourselves. When we don't take time for our rest, we can become scattered and cranky. Lots of studies show that teenagers in particular do not get enough sleep; with college students it's even worse. Do you take time to rest? Is Sunday a day of rest for you? If not, could it be?

God, I want to care for myself as much as you care for me.

For more: Even Jesus needed rest. See John, chapters 6 and 7, in which he keeps trying to go off to be by himself.

You have become dull in [hearing]. (Hebrews 5:11)

Have you become dull in hearing? It is possible to listen and not hear. This happens particularly when we think we have heard it all before. Do you mentally "check out" a lot when you are supposedly listening? Do things go in one ear and out the other? Might God be saying something that you are not hearing? Challenge yourself to be a better listener today.

May I be more aware of the people and of you speaking to me today, God.

For more: Some people listen to God and then choose not to hear. Read Psalm 95.

September 18

Let us . . . lay aside every weight and the sin that clings so closely, and let us run with perseverance that race that is set before us. (Hebrews 12:1)

We know it: we are all sinners. Sometimes sinfulness can be overwhelming, especially when it is pointed out repeatedly. But we need to remember that in spite of our sins, God offers us salvation through the life, death, and Resurrection of Christ. So when you are feeling burdened by failures, worries, or sin, remember this passage. God wants us to focus on our life with God, not hang on to our problems.

I know that I disappoint you sometimes, God. Help me to put aside my sin and to focus on your goodness and the goodness you have put in me.

For more: See Deuteronomy 30:19.

In the midst of a busy life, [the rich man] will wither away. (James 1:11)

The more "stuff" we have, the more time we spend with our stuff, both using it and taking care of it. Eventually, if we have too much stuff, we will be swallowed up and lost in it. For example, a car demands maintenance. We can't just drive it without changing the oil, filling the tires, or flushing the radiator. Stuff in itself is not bad, but too much stuff can cause us to lose ourselves.

May I never become too focused on my stuff, O God.

For more: See a similar text in Matthew 6:19–21.

September 20

One person is tempted by one's own desire. (James 1:14)

We each have wants: wanting things or wanting situations to be different. But this passage warns us to be cautious of our wants. Sometimes our wants are fueled by our own selfishness or insecurity. At other times our desires can be calls by God to do God's work. Pay attention to your wants. Where are they coming from?

God, you are wisdom. Give me wisdom, that I may understand my own desires.

For more: Jacob was led by his desire for something that belonged to his brother. Read about it in Genesis 25:19–34.

THE APOSTLE MATTHEW

As Jesus was walking along, he saw a man called Matthew sitting at the tax booth; and he said to him, "Follow me." And he got up and followed him. (Matthew 9:9)

Today is the feast of Matthew, one of the disciples of Jesus that we know by name. Jesus called Matthew, and Matthew chose to respond. What would you do if you were standing by your locker between classes and Jesus came up and said, "Follow me"? Would you leave your friends and school behind and go where he led you?

Jesus, help me to follow you, no matter the cost.

For more: See the final chapter of John, where Jesus gives more instructions for how to follow him.

September 22

Be doers of the word, and not merely hearers. (James 1:22)

We might hear the Gospel fairly regularly, whether in church, at home, or in our own prayer. But being a hearer of the Gospel is not enough. Jesus calls us to be doers. The Scriptures are not intended to be a self-help book or a collection of wise stories. They are a call to a way of life. The next time you hear the word, ask yourself, What is this asking me to do?

God, I want to be a hearer and a doer.

For more: Read the story of the good Samaritan (Luke 10:29–37), the story of a true doer.

You will show me the path that leads to life; your presence fills me with joy, and your help brings pleasure forever. (Psalm 16:11)

Following the path of life, the path that leads to God, may mean hardship, and it usually challenges us. However it also means great joy and pleasure. The psalmist recognizes this. Keeping God's promise of joy in mind can help us too. What are the joys and pleasures that you have received already from God?

Joyful God, to follow your path means many things. May I always remember that your way leads to joy and pleasure. You are the God of life and all good things.

September 24

My child, keep your father's commandment, and do not forsake your mother's teaching. (Proverbs 6:20)

This is simply a restatement of the fourth commandment, but it is a good reminder of the ideal attitude toward our parent(s) or guardian(s). Although it may not always be apparent to us, parents and guardians usually try to act out of love, and they often have a wisdom that we do not have. How can you work harder to show your respect and love for your parent(s) or guardian(s)?

God, you are both mother and father to us. Help us to be your good children and to respect and listen to our parent(s) or guardian(s). May we strive to follow their word and not to disappoint them.

A sensible person will not overlook a thoughtful suggestion. (Sirach 32:18)

What a simple and practical bit of advice. When someone, especially someone we know and respect, gives us a suggestion, we should probably pay attention. That is a sensible thing to do, although pride can get in the way. Has anyone given you a thoughtful suggestion in the last day or two? Did you accept this person's help? Could you now if you didn't then?

God, it is all too easy for me to get defensive when someone suggests something to me. Help me to be open to the help others can offer, and let me be grateful for the practical advice I do receive from others.

September 26

As long as the earth endures, seedtime and harvest, cold and heat, summer and winter, day and night, shall not cease. (Genesis 8:22)

This is part of the promise God made to Noah after the flood. It is a reassuring promise, letting us know that the familiar cycles of nature that we count on will continue, despite the natural disasters that occur. How would your life be different without the change of seasons?

Creator of all life, thank you for all your promises, but especially for the cycles of nature that I often take for granted and yet count on. They are a sign of your providential love for us.

VINCENT DE PAUL (1580–1660)

Quick to be generous, they give to the poor; their righteousness stands firm forever. (Psalm 112:9)

Many of us have a Vincent de Paul Center in our city or town. It is a place where we can drop off food and clothing for needy people. Vincent is the patron of all charitable societies. He devoted much of his life to helping establish church groups to provide spiritual and physical relief to poor and sick people. He once said, "Cherish the poor . . . since Our Lord is in them and they in Our Lord." Think about contacting the Vincent de Paul Society or a similar agency in your area to volunteer your help.

God present in the poor, help us to realize that serving the needs of others is something all of us are called to do. Let us be generous in giving to others. Let us give not only of our surplus but also of our time and energy.

September 28

Some friends play at friendship but a true friend sticks closer than one's nearest kin. (Proverbs 18:24)

We've all had friends who "play" at being friends. They're friends as long as it is fun or it somehow benefits them. But when times get rough or the fun stops, they're gone. True friends are still there, standing by your side. Treasure those friendships, and resolve to be a true friend yourself, no matter what.

God, my faithful friend, thank you for the gift of true friends. Help me to treat my friends well and to be a true friend myself. Let me never forget that you are always at my side, the truest friend of all.

ARCHANGELS MICHAEL, GABRIEL, RAPHAEL

Bless Yahweh, all angels, mighty in strength to enforce God's word. (Psalm 103:20)

Only three angels are mentioned by name in the Bible: Michael, Gabriel, and Raphael. Each of their names ends in *el,* which is an ancient name for God. Michael protects, Gabriel announces, and Raphael guides, and the three of them witness to the many ways that angels, God's special messengers, are part of our lives.

O God, certainly angels are among us, guiding us, protecting us, and giving us glimpses of your loving concern for us. May I be an earthly angel for others as well, and help them to know of your presence.

For more: To find more about these three angels, see Revelation, chapter 12; Luke, chapter 1; and the Book of Tobit.

September 30

For where your treasure is, there your heart will be also. (Matthew 6:21)

When a tornado levels a town or a flood sweeps away houses, the victims often tell reporters that the hardest things to lose are personal items: family photo albums, gifts from grandparents, and so on. We can tell a great deal about ourselves when we look at what we treasure most. If you could keep only three of your current belongings, what would they be? What would this say about you?

God, I want to set my heart on you. Thank you for the gifts of faith and love that you continuously share with me. Please don't let me become so attached to my things that I forget to treasure you.

For more: Read Luke 12:13–34 to see what Jesus recommends that we treasure.

THÉRÈSE OF LISIEUX (1873–1897)

For I have set you an example, that you also should do as I have done to you. (John 13:15)

Thérèse lived a hidden life as a contemplative nun, died of tuberculosis at the age of twenty-four, and yet became one of the most popular Catholic saints because of her simple spirituality. She remarked, "I've got to take myself just as I am, with all my imperfections; but somehow I shall have to find out a little way, all my own." Her "little way" came to mean doing even small acts with as much care and love as she could and offering them to God. Do one of your everyday tasks with great care, and offer it to God today.

God of love, today I offer this everyday task of mine to you. As I do it, I wonder at how you have given me the ability to do this small thing, and I ask you to accept it as my gift of thanksgiving for all that you have done for me.

For more: Read John 13:1–20 to see how Jesus taught the Apostles to serve one another in love.

GUARDIAN ANGELS

God has commanded angels to guard you in all your ways. (Psalm 91:11)

God's angels are everywhere. Angels are the messengers of God, showing up in unexpected places and times. We even see images of them on T-shirts, backpacks, and coffee mugs! Would you recognize an angel if you met one?

Holy One, thank you for watching over me and for sending angels to guide and guard me. Help me to remember that my guardian angel travels with me everywhere I go.

For more: Look in Genesis, chapter 32, to see how one young man wrestled with an angel and gained a blessing.

Yahweh, you search me and know me. (Psalm 139:1)

Sometimes we feel as though nobody really knows us or even cares to know us. But God always does. Even when we fool ourselves into believing that God doesn't, God still does. All through this day, consider that God is walking right beside you. Do you see things differently?

All-knowing God, thank you for caring enough about me to know me deep in my heart. Help me to remember that even when I feel discouraged or misunderstood, you know and care how I feel.

For more: Jesus promises to be with us always. Read his last words to the disciples in Matthew 28:16–20.

FRANCIS OF ASSISI (1181–1226)

Praise God from the heavens, . . . mountains and all you hills, you fruit trees and all you cedars, you wild beasts and all tame animals, you creeping things and flying birds. (Psalm 148:1,9–10)

Francis of Assisi remains one of the most popular and best-loved saints. His image can be seen in countless gardens, where he is depicted surrounded by animals. Francis loved nature and saw it as a reflection of God's glory. He gave up a wealthy life to follow God in utter simplicity and with a joyful, humble heart. He constantly reminds us of the need to live simply and close to nature.

"O Divine Master, grant that I may seek not so much to be consoled as to console, to be understood as to understand, to be loved as to love; for it is in giving that we receive, in pardoning that we are pardoned, and in dying that we are born to eternal life." (Francis of Assisi)

Surely God is my salvation; I will trust, and will not be afraid. (Isaiah 12:2)

Fear can sure keep us from doing things. When we are afraid, we become paralyzed and we can't act. When we trust that God is in control of the world, we let go of our fear and enter into a whole new world of trust and openness to God's way of salvation. The next time you feel afraid, try to go beyond the fear and trust God to help you.

Trustworthy God, you have promised to be with me everywhere I go. Because of your promise, I have no reason to fear. Accept my fears and strengthen me in trust, so that I will be able to act freely and choose wisely to follow your way of salvation.

October 6

But even if you do suffer for doing what is right, you are blessed. (1 Peter 3:14)

Sometimes doing the right thing means going against the rules. And yet we live in a system of rules, so doing the right thing may mean that we will need to suffer as we accept the consequences of our actions. Dr. Martin Luther King Jr. is one great example of righteous suffering. He spent time in prison and ultimately died for defying immoral, racist laws. What would you do if you were confronted with a law that you thought was wrong?

God, I know that you suffer with all the suffering people. Give me strength when I am confronted with difficult situations.

For more: The disciple Paul spent much time in prison because he was preaching the news of Jesus. See the Letter to Philemon, written from prison.

Beloved, let us love one another, because love is from God. (1 John 4:7)

As limited humans we cannot totally understand what God is like, but we can get a good idea from our own experience and from Jesus. There is a lot we don't know, but we do know that God is love. So for us, to love is to be like God. Who are the people you love? When you love do you feel the goodness of God in you? Do you see it in those you love?

God whose name is Love, thank you for loving me and for giving me the ability to love others. May I become more like you.

For more: Read the fourth chapter of James, on the love of God and its relation to us.

October 8

I cried to you for help, my God, and you healed me. (Psalm 30:2)

God created us with wonderful, automatic healing systems within our own body: for example, our immune system and our blood that instantly begins to clot when we're cut. When we pray for healing, we should probably pray that we will do all we can to help what God has already created us to do: heal. So when you are sick, consider praying for God's help to sleep more, to eat better, or to exercise more.

Divine Healer, so often we turn to you in times of illness, and we want to be healed quickly. Thank you for all the times you have healed us through the natural healing wonders that you created in us and thank you for the special graces you send.

Keep your heart with all vigilance, for from it flow the springs of life. (Proverbs 4:23)

What is inside your heart right now? What is going on within you? This verse reminds us to be attentive to what is going on in our heart, to the quality of life springing forth from us.

God, so often you speak to us in our heart. Let me keep my heart attentive to you and directed toward your love. Keep the springs of life that flow from me full of positive energy.

October 10

This is love, that we walk according to his commandments. (2 John 1:6)

And what are the commandments? Well, the two key ones are to love God and to love our neighbors as ourselves. So love means to love. To love implies kindness, charity, justice, and so on. Loving isn't easy, but God's grace makes it possible.

God, I want to obey you out of love. I want to love. Teach me how.

For more: See Romans, chapter 7.

Turn away from evil and practice good; seek peace and follow after it. (Psalm 34:14)

Simple words, but such profound advice! We are counseled not only to seek peace but to pursue it. How willing are you to put your energy into making peace? Do you need to make peace with anyone? How can you seek peace with her or him?

God, help me to be a peacemaker who actively pursues peace in all areas of my life. Help me make peace with (name of person). May I always strive to do what is peaceful.

October 12

"I am the Alpha and the Omega," says the Lord God, who is and who was and who is to come, the Almighty. (Revelation 1:8)

I am the beginning (the Alpha) and the end (the Omega), says God. God always has been and always will be. There is nothing that God has not seen or experienced. Therefore there is nothing in your heart or your life that surprises God and that God cannot handle. Turn to God with all your heart, and God can get you through anything.

God, I know you have been and will always be, and that you will always be with me. Help me to trust that.

For more: If you are hesitant about turning to God, read Psalm 69.

Refrain from anger and forsake wrath! Fret not; it tends only to evil. (Psalm 37:8)

Think of the last time you were angry. How did you deal with your anger? Did you fret over it? How can you redirect your anger into something positive?

God, I often find myself stewing over something that's happened, and often I let anger take over. Help me to avoid anger and wishing evil on others. Teach me to forgive and to let go of anger.

October 14

Look, I have set before you an open door, which no one is able to shut. (Revelation 3:8)

We have a God who loves us and who has given us the gift of faith. We have an open door to a relationship with God. God wants to know us and wants to be known by us. If that were not the case, God would not have sent Jesus to us. You can walk through the door by means of prayer, Scripture study, and service. Are you willing to walk through the door?

I want to know you, God, and I want you to know me.

For more: See Romans 8:31–35. With God all things are possible!

A generous person will be enriched, and one who gives water will get water. (Proverbs 11:25)

The good we do is like the act of planting seeds. Eventually the good we do will come back to nourish us. How can you be more generous today?

God, help us to be generous people. Let us share whatever we have with others, confident that good will return to us.

October 16

[God] will wipe every tear from their eyes. Death will be no more; mourning and crying and pain will be no more, for the first things have passed away. (Revelation 21:4)

Sometimes life is horrible: things don't go right for us, unfair things happen, people we love die for seemingly no reason. Jesus teaches that when our life on earth ends, we will see our God face-to-face. When we are with God, all we will know is joy. Have you lost someone you love? Do you think of them as being happy with God? It doesn't fill the absence in our life, but sometimes it helps to think that they are happier than we can ever imagine.

I want to believe in the joy that all will know with you someday, God.

For more: Death has no sting for us. See 1 Corinthians 15:55.

I have loved you with an everlasting love; therefore I have continued my faithfulness to you. (Jeremiah 31:3)

God's love for us will never cease. Despite our unfaithfulness God will always be faithful to us. How can you be more faithful to God?

God, your love and faithfulness are overwhelming. Thank you for the reminder that you have loved us always and will continue to do so. Help us to reflect your love to others.

THE APOSTLE LUKE

In the first book, Theophilus, I wrote about all that Jesus did and taught from the beginning until the day when he was taken up to heaven, after giving instructions through the Holy Spirit to the apostles whom he had chosen. (Acts of the Apostles 1:1–2)

Luke is one of the four Gospel writers, or Evangelists, of the New Testament, but unlike the others, he also wrote a second volume entitled the Acts of the Apostles. Luke's Gospel emphasizes the compassion of Jesus and his concern for women, the outcasts, and the marginalized. Luke was a companion of Paul and, according to legend, a physician, so he often pictures Jesus and Paul as healers.

God of healing, God of light, come and heal what is broken within me. Bring me your light to fill the dark places in my soul.

I am not ashamed of the gospel. (Romans 1:16)

Sometimes we may take heat for our religious beliefs. People may laugh at us for belonging to a church, for taking part in church activities, and so on. Why do some people try to make us ashamed of the Gospel? Have you ever felt that way?

It's not always easy, dear God, to be a follower of yours. Help me to carry my faith with me when I speak and in all my actions.

For more: Peter learned the hard way; see John 18:25–27.

October 20

Better is the little that the just have than the abundance of the wicked. (Psalm 37:16)

We live in a nation that pushes us to think of abundance as having lots of possessions. We can never have too many cars or varieties of soda or even too much fun. But where does it stop? How many of your possessions possess you? What do you really need to be happy?

God, I know that I can't take anything with me when I leave this earth. I also know that a righteous person is what you call me to be. Help me to resist the urge to acquire more and more, and let me learn the freedom of living simply.

You are worthy, our Lord and God, to receive glory and honor and power, for you created all things, and by your will they existed and were created. (Revelation 4:11)

God created absolutely everything and everyone that we know. Make a special point to take a look around and appreciate God's work today. All of it is extraordinary.

God, your world is beautiful. I hope that I will always appreciate and care for it.

For more: Read the creation story in the first chapter of Genesis.

October 22

After this, I saw four angels standing at the four corners of the earth. (Revelation 7:1)

If we believe that God dwells in every one of us through the Spirit and works through us—as the Gospel teaches—then we are all angels of sorts, for we are messengers of God. Revelation tells us that God sent angels to the four corners of the earth. God gave us a beautiful gift in our planet, and sent both us and the angels to care for it. Shouldn't it be our job to protect the earth? Do you recycle? Do you conserve energy? What else can you do to protect our earth?

Help us all to care for the earth, creator God, and to see it as you do, for you said that it is good.

For more: Read the other creation story in the second chapter of Genesis.

Whoever loves discipline loves knowledge, but those who hate to be rebuked are stupid. (Proverbs 12:1)

Some strong words about discipline here. But they are true, aren't they? To truly learn anything, we need discipline. When we refuse to accept correction, we only show our stupidity and our resistance to learning and growing as a person. Ask yourself: Do I love learning? Do I welcome help?

God, the root word of *discipline* is *disciple,* which is what you call each of us to be. We need to learn how to follow you better. Help me to be a better disciple, learner, and student.

October 24

I confess my iniquity; I am sorry for my sin. (Psalm 38:18)

Some guilt over doing wrong is a good thing. It means we have an active conscience. The only way to clear our conscience is to confess our sorrow to God. What are you truly sorry for at this moment? Take a few moments to confess your sins to God. If you feel that you can, you may want to make peace with someone that you offended. A fresh start does wonders!

God, I need to be honest with you about my failings and the many times I have turned away from you. Give me the courage to admit to my sins and to resolve to do better.

Whoever does not provide for relatives, and especially family members, has denied the faith. (1 Timothy 5:8)

Do you provide for your family? We tend to think of providing as a financial issue, but we provide for one another in many ways. To provide is to enable someone to grow and flourish. Do you provide for your family? Do you support and encourage your siblings or parent(s), or do you tear them down and make fun of them? Be intentional about providing for your family today.

God, help me to provide for my family as you have provided for me.

For more: Read about Mary providing for her pregnant cousin Elizabeth in Luke, chapter 1.

October 26

Do not add to the troubles of the desperate, or delay giving to the needy. (Sirach 4:3)

This seems like rather obvious advice, doesn't it? And yet sometimes we add to the troubles of other people by comments we make or by refusing to help them, or worse, by simply pretending that they don't exist. How can you help someone out today and make her or his life better?

God, why is it so hard for me to help others? Help me to resist the urge to turn away, to look in the other direction. Help me to not put off the good that I can do. I may not have the chance tomorrow.

For the love of money is the root of all kinds of evils. (1 Timothy 6:10)

In this text the Scriptures make a subtle but important distinction for us. It is not money that is the root of all evils, but the love of money. We get into trouble when we value money and things above everything else. What do you value most in life? Where does money rank in your list of what's important?

For more: See what else the Scriptures have to say about money in Matthew 19:16–30.

THE APOSTLES SIMON AND JUDE

And when day came, [Jesus] called his disciples and chose twelve of them, whom he also named apostles: Simon, whom he named Peter, and his brother Andrew, and James, and John, and Philip, and Bartholomew, and Matthew, and Thomas, and James son of Alphaeus, and Simon, who was called the Zealot, and Judas son of James, and Judas Iscariot, who became a traitor. (Luke 6:13–16)

The two Apostles we celebrate today are Simon the Zealot and Judas, the son of James. Zealots were members of a Jewish nationalist group who wanted to bring down Roman rule. Judas is referred to as Jude in English to distinguish him from Judas Iscariot. Other than their names, there are no direct references to Simon and Jude in the rest of the Bible. Though they are not famous Apostles, Jesus called them and must have loved them—just as he does you.

Holy One, we thank you today for the Simons and the Judes of the world. They are not the stars or the popular heroes, but they remain loyal and are good followers. They are an essential part of your Reign here on earth.

God is our refuge and our strength, our ever-present help in distress. (Psalm 46:1)

Spend some time reflecting on God as an "ever-present help." What does that mean? How is God ever-present to you?

God, you are indeed my strength. I turn to you in times of trouble and you are there, even though at times I struggle to sense your presence. Help me to realize that you are always present, especially when things get rough.

October 30

The Spirit of the Lord is upon me, because he has anointed me. (Luke 4:18)

In the Hebrew Scriptures, a person who is chosen to do something is anointed. The anointing with oil symbolizes that the person is special. Today Christians are all anointed through baptism to signal that they have been chosen to do God's work. How are you being called? Do you feel as if you are chosen?

Thank you for choosing me to do your work, living and true God.

For more: Read about when Jesus was anointed (Luke 7:36–50) and about the anointing of David (First Samuel, chapter 16).

HALLOWEEN

Do not let your hearts be troubled. Believe in God, believe also in me. In my Father's house, there are many dwelling places. (John 14:1–2)

Halloween comes from "All Hallows' Evening." All Hallows was an old name for tomorrow's feast of All Saints' Day. We still use the word *hallow* whenever we say the Lord's Prayer: "hallowed (or "holy") be your name." As with most Christian feasts, the observance begins the evening before, which accounts for the name of this All Saints' Eve, or Halloween.

Holy One, even though Halloween has lost most of its original meaning, we know that there is nothing to be afraid of. The powers of darkness will not conquer you or us. You have assured us of that. Thank you, God, our savior.

November 1

ALL SAINTS' DAY

Beloved, we are God's children now; what we will be has not yet been revealed. What we do know is this: when he is revealed, we will be like him. (1 John 3:2)

Naming people "saints" acknowledges that they led holy lives, did the work of God, and are now with God. A saint is anyone who lives with God, whether officially recognized or not. Many of us have known saints. Take time today to remember those special people in your life who have gone on to be with God. Who are the saints in your life? Are you a better person because of them?

I know that you work through many people, God. Thank you for all your saints and for the work they have done in your name.

For more: Read Psalm 116—I will walk in the presence of the Lord in the land of the living!

ALL SOULS' DAY

The souls of the righteous are in the hand of God, and no torment will ever touch them. In the eyes of the foolish they seemed to have died, and their departure was thought to be a disaster, and their going from us their destruction; but they are at peace. (Wisdom of Solomon 3:1–3)

Today we remember and pray for all those who have died and gone before us. As a Christian community, we are all one body. Take some time to remember and to pray for those persons in your life who have passed away.

O God, on this special day, I pray for all the faithful departed, especially (names of persons). May they rest in peace.

November 3

You created my inmost being and knit me together in my mother's womb. (Psalm 139:13)

We have all seen images of unborn babies. We may know the scientific explanation about how babies develop in the nine months of pregnancy from a single cell to a complex human being. This psalm passage gives us an image of God's loving role in forming us. Reflect on the sacredness of life, especially life in the womb.

God, you have fashioned each of us, and life is your gift. Forgive me my failure to reverence all life, especially my own. May I respect my life and that of all creation.

For more: Read and reflect on all of Psalm 139.

My thoughts are not your thoughts, nor are your ways my ways, says the Lord. (Isaiah 55:8)

This message from God seems rather obvious, but we sometimes act as if we know God's ways and understand what makes God "tick." Are you ever tempted to think that you have "a corner on God"?

God, in the end, despite all the theology and sermons and books, you remain a mystery to me. Forgive me my arrogance in assuming I know how you think. Give me the gift of humility in your presence.

November 5

All my close friends are watching for me to stumble. (Jeremiah 20:10)

Have you ever felt this way? The prophet Jeremiah is tired of serving God and feels that everyone is just waiting for him to make a mistake. Why are we so eager at times to see someone close to us fail? Give a friend some encouragement today.

God, it is not always easy to follow you. Jeremiah knew that, as did many others. Give me the courage to persevere despite the unkindness I feel in those around me. Let me always strive to build up other people.

For more: Read Jeremiah 20:7–18.

My child, give me your heart, and let your eyes observe my ways. (Proverbs 23:26)

God asks for nothing less than our heart, the symbolic center of our love and feelings. Does anything prevent you from giving your heart to God?

God, help me to be wholehearted in my faith and to observe your works and goodness in our world. Keep my attention focused on you as I go through this day. Help me to give my heart to you.

November 7

Praise God, sun and moon; praise God, all you shining stars. (Psalm 148:3)

Whenever we look at the sky, we see reminders of God's glory and infinite majesty. That is especially true in the night sky. How do the sun, moon, and stars reflect the glory and majesty of God?

God, thank you for the heavenly reminders of your majesty, for the lights in the sky that seem to point to your glory. May I never lose my sense of wonder or awe at your great works.

What does the Lord require of you but to do justice, and to love kindness, and to walk humbly with your God? (Micah 6:8)

This is quite a summons for each of us. How do you "do justice" in your daily life? Do you truly love kindness? How do you walk humbly with your God?

God, this day I ask you to help me to act justly, to love tenderly, and to strive to walk humbly with you. Teach me how.

November 9

[God] alone is my rock, my stronghold, my fortress: I stand firm. (Psalm 62:2)

Ponder how God is a rock, a stronghold, and a fortress for you. Consider asking someone a lot older—maybe a grandparent—about how God has been a fortress for her or him.

God, you are many things to many people. Each of us approaches you from a different angle, and the Scriptures present us with many images of both power and tenderness. None of these images captures you fully, but each of them helps us to center on you. Continue to inspire us with images and symbols that help us know you better.

I will instruct you and show you the way you should walk; I will counsel you and watch over you. (Psalm 32:8)

Another important image of God is that of guide or teacher who shows us the right path. Notice that God counsels. God does not force us or push us but counsels us. What sort of counsel or guidance do you need from the One True Guide?

Lead me, holy Counselor, to know what to do with my life, how to make good decisions, and how to live life fully.

The Lord opened [Lydia's] heart to listen eagerly to what was said by Paul. (Acts of the Apostles 16:14)

Lydia came to know Jesus through the words and deeds of Paul, for she lived after the time of Jesus. We too live after the time of Jesus, for we are not actual witnesses to his life here on earth. Who are the people who told you about Jesus? What would your life look like if those people had never told you?

Gentle God, thank you for the people who have taught me about you and about your Son, Jesus. I am grateful for the gift of faith.

For more: Read about the original witness, John the Baptist, in Matthew 3:7–10.

Now it was Mary Magdalene, Joanna, Mary the mother of James, and the other women with them who told this to the apostles. But these words seemed to them an idle tale, and they did not believe them. (Luke 24:10–11)

It was the women who first found and believed in the resurrected Jesus, and yet no one believed them. The women persisted, and finally the Apostles believed. We are called to be like Joanna, Mary, and Mary Magdalene, readily sharing the Good News. Do you know someone who could benefit from you sharing your hope, faith, and charity? They may not believe you at first, but great things might happen if you keep talking!

Give me courage to share my faith, especially with those who most need to hear about it.

For more: Read the whole story of the Resurrection (John, chapter 20) and of how Jesus appeared to his followers.

FRANCES CABRINI (1850–1917)

The human mind plans the way, but the Lord directs the steps. (Proverbs 16:9)

Mother Cabrini was born in Italy, came to New York, and with the community of sisters she founded, served the Italian immigrants there and went on to found sixty-seven schools, orphanages, and hospitals in the United States, Latin America, and Europe. She crossed the ocean thirty times, and she rode a mule across the Andes, spreading the Good News. She declared, "Let our hands . . . do the work of a hundred hands and bring His love and aid to the lost souls . . . wherever [there] is suffering." She is the patron of immigrants.

God of all creation, one determined person can accomplish great things with your help. Help me, in the spirit of Mother Cabrini, reach out to those who are new to our nation and way of life. May I be extra sensitive to their needs.

November 14

Pray then in this way: Our Father . . . (Matthew 6:9)

The Our Father, or the Lord's Prayer, is prayed by Christians everywhere. It is a prayer given to us by Jesus. Pray the Our Father now. What are we saying to God and asking of God when we pray this prayer?

Loving God, may my prayer to you always be intentional and sincere. Help me to focus.

For more: Read the sixth chapter of Matthew and the eleventh chapter of Luke, where Jesus teaches us the Our Father.

November 15

Our Father . . . (Matthew 6:9)

How amazing it is that we call this awesome God "Father." That speaks volumes about our relationship with the Divine and about how much we are loved. Paul says, "When we cry 'Abba! Father!' it is that very Spirit bearing witness with our spirit that we are children of God" (Romans 8:15–16). Even more surprising, *Abba* is best translated as "Daddy" or "Poppa." What does it mean to you to call God "Father" or "Abba"?

Our Poppa
Our Mother
Our Creator
Our Friend

For more: Read the story of the prodigal son (Luke 15:11–32). This is a wonderful metaphor for God as Poppa! The preceding story in Luke of the woman looking for a lost coin is the same story with a different metaphor, God as Momma.

Our Father in heaven. (Matthew 6:9)

Where exactly is God? Christians believe that God can be found throughout all creation. God dwells in the heart of those who love, and having God live within us is heaven. The love we give and receive in our everyday life is a glimpse of heaven.

Our Father in heaven
    And on the earth
    And with the oppressed
    And among sinners

For more: God signified a sacred space in the third chapter of Exodus. The ground was so holy, Moses had to take off his shoes!

November 17

Hallowed be your name. (Matthew 6:9)

Hallowed, or holy, is your name, O God! Does the idea of God or the name of God do anything to you? Does it make you stop and think about this amazing power that is at the center of your faith? How can we make ourselves more aware of the true holiness of the name of God?

Hallowed be your name
    Awe-inspiring your presence
    Wondrous your image
    Revered be your love

For more: Read Philippians 2:9–11. It talks about the holiness and importance of a name.

Your kingdom come. (Matthew 6:10)

With these words we make a pledge to bring about God's Reign by peacemaking, service, justice, and charity. These words ask God for the grace to keep our pledge. How can you help bring about God's Reign?

Your kingdom come
    God, bring us home
    Grant us assurance
    Give us safety

For more: Jesus paints many pictures of the Kingdom of heaven in Matthew, chapter 13. Check it out, for this is what we're praying for!

November 19

Your will be done. (Matthew 6:10)

We pledge to do God's will: that is, to love God and our neighbor. The evil in the world exists because God's will is not being done. Stories of rebellion against God's will dominate the evening news in the forms of violence, hatred, and prejudice. How do you want to do God's will today?

Your will be done
Through peace
Through love
Through justice

For more: Jesus battled Satan. In Matthew 16:23, he tells Satan to get behind him.

On earth. (Matthew 6:10)

We pray that God's will be done on earth for everyone, not just ourselves. The idea is that when God's Reign is established, the whole earth will be heaven. What is your role on this earth to ensure that this happens?

On earth
    In the streets
    In all shelters
    In our lives

The last few hours of Jesus' human life are difficult to read about (Mark 14:36, Matthew 26:39, Luke 22:42, and John 12:27). Doing the will of God was not easy for Jesus.

November 21

As it is in heaven. (Matthew 6:10)

Jesus tells us that our world should look like heaven! What does heaven look like? Heaven is when we are united with God, when all life makes sense, when all God's people live fully, are loved, have hope, and can believe. Do you ever take time to think about what it will be like when you are united with your God? Ponder that.

As it is in heaven
 Unconditional love
 Freely giving
 Everlasting peace

For more: See Genesis, chapter 2, for a small hint of paradise.

Give us this day our daily bread. (Matthew 6:11)

Here we acknowledge that everything we have is a gift from God. This prayer is for the needs of the whole human family: Give "us," not just "me," daily bread. We are asking God to give *us* everything we need. The prayer also recalls that our souls need the Bread of Life, Jesus.

Give us this day our daily bread
  Sustenance
  Challenge
  Contentment

For more: Read Matthew 6:24–25. Our God does know what we need!

November 23

And forgive us our debts. (Matthew 6:12)

Many of us have had it pounded into our head that we are sinners! And yet how often do we stop to think about our sins, for we sin daily? We need healing and forgiveness. God will forgive us, but we need to ask. What sins have you committed that you need forgiveness for?

And forgive us our debts
    Our jealousies
    Our pettiness
    Our thanklessness

For more: See the parable of the unforgiving servant (Matthew 18:23–35).

As we also have forgiven our debtors. (Matthew 6:12)

Jesus gave us the golden rule: "You shall love your neighbor as yourself" (Matthew 19:19). We are asking God to treat us as we have treated our friends who betray us, our classmates who make fun of us or ignore us, our neighbors who gossip about us. Have we treated these people the way we want God to treat us? Is there someone you need to forgive?

As we also have forgiven our debtors
 Our neighbors
 Our enemies
 Our friends

For more: The disciple Paul persecuted Christians before his conversion and was later forgiven by the community. See Acts of the Apostles 9:1–19.

November 25

And lead us not into temptation. (Matthew 6:13)

A better translation of the original Greek is "and do not allow us to enter into temptation." Temptations always appear as good things; that is why we are drawn to them. But temptations are lies. In many ways asking God to keep us away from temptation is like asking God for wisdom and guidance to recognize potential trouble. God is more than willing, but we need to take time to talk to and to listen to God. Do you pray when you need advice? It might help.

And lead us not into temptation
    Guide us
    Show us the way
    Take us beyond ourselves

For more: See what Jesus says about temptation in Mark 9:42–50.

But deliver us from evil. (Matthew 6:13)

We know evil exists. Our challenge is to steer clear of it. Before we can avoid it, however, we need to recognize it, for it comes in many disguises. Is there evil in your life? Do you participate in evil, however unintentionally? What behaviors or habits do you need to be delivered from?

But deliver us from evil
Greed
Power
Control

For more: David didn't recognize evil until Nathan pointed it out to him. See Second Samuel, chapters 11 and 12 (especially 12:7).

November 27

Yahweh guards you, shades you. With Yahweh at your right hand the sun cannot harm you. (Psalm 121:5–6)

It may seem strange to think of God as shade, and yet think of what shade represents. It is what we seek when we are hot, it protects us from the glare of the sun, and it is a cool and refreshing place to be. Being in the shade can rejuvenate us. Isn't that what God's grace does as well?

God, we thank you for keeping us close to you, for being our shade in the glare of daily life. Refresh me often, and let me seek your shade eagerly.

How often have I desired to gather your children together as a hen gathers her brood under her wings. (Matthew 23:37)

God gathers all Christians together much as a mother gathers her children. We all belong together, and we all belong to God. Christians live in Japan, Russia, Angola, Saudi Arabia—all over the globe. We are part of a world church. Spend some time today praying for Christians throughout the world. Someday we will all be under the same wings.

I pray in thanksgiving for Christians around the world today, God, especially for those who are not free to openly worship you.

For more: Read 2 Corinthians 1:1–11—we are called to be aware of all members of the Body of Christ.

DOROTHY DAY
(1897–1980)

Those who are generous are blessed, for they share their bread with the poor. (Proverbs 22:9)

Catholic Worker Houses or Dorothy Day Centers exist in many cities. These are places where the needy can be ministered to. The person behind this movement was Dorothy Day, an amazing woman who converted to Catholicism after the birth of her daughter and who cofounded the Catholic Worker Movement. She devoted her long life to serving the poor, promoting peace, and working for social justice. She is a twentieth-century prophet who lived what she spoke about: "Christ is always with us, always asking for room in our hearts."

Just and loving God, you call each of us to serve others. Dorothy Day responded to that call, but went much further. She worked for social change, never losing sight of the core message of the Gospel. Help us to realize we are all called to share our bread with poor people.

Likewise the Spirit helps us in our weakness. (Romans 8:26)

For a lot of reasons, many of us question our abilities, talents, skills, intelligence, and looks. But we never grow or make a contribution in life unless we use all of who we are. The spirit of God works within us, helping us in our weakness and encouraging us in our strength. Do you have gifts that could be developed? The Spirit will help you in your weakness.

God, I know you sometimes ask me to do things I may not be comfortable with. Help me to trust that the Spirit will give me help in my weakness so that I may become all that I am capable of being.

For more: Read Psalm 121—our help comes from God.

WORLD AIDS DAY

While he was in one of the cities, there came a man full of leprosy; and when he saw Jesus, he fell on his face and besought him, "Lord, if you will, you can make me clean." And he stretched out his hand and touched him saying, "I will; be clean." (Luke 5:12–13)

Today is World AIDS Day, a day to remember those who live with AIDS, those who have died of the disease, and those who love and care for them. Despite advances in treatment, most people with the disease still die of its complications. Christ calls us to love and pray for those who have been affected. AIDS is not a disease that anyone deserves, but everyone that has it deserves to be loved. Take a minute and pray for someone, maybe someone you know, that has been affected by HIV or AIDS.

God of all, be with those who suffer the ravages of AIDS. May they find comfort in you and in me.

For more: Read the story of the lepers in Luke 5:12–16, substituting the word AIDS for leprosy. Does that change the story for you at all?

Do you see persons wise in their own eyes? There is more hope for fools than for them. (Proverbs 26:12)

What does it mean to be wise? Why is it unwise for us to presume that we are wise? Reflect on this for a bit. Why would a truly wise person not consider himself or herself wise?

God, I thank you for the gift of wisdom and especially for those who possess it in abundance. Help me to seek the wisdom of others and never to presume to be wise myself, but instead always to be willing to learn.

December 3

Prepare the way of the Lord! (Isaiah 40:3, Matthew 3:3)

Every year we hear this message in the early days of Advent. "Prepare the way of the Lord!" What does this mean for your life? What can you do to prepare the way? What do you want to do to make this Advent a time of preparation that goes beyond shopping, wrapping gifts, and eating?

This time before Christmas is a crazy time, loving God. Help me to slow down and learn the true meaning of Jesus' coming, that I may prepare my heart.

For more: Read Isaiah, chapter 40, one of the most well known Advent texts.

How good it is, how pleasant, for God's people to live in unity. (Psalm 133:1)

How well does your family get along? How about the other relatives? It is indeed a blessing when families get along. How can you help bring your family closer together?

God, bless my family, especially as we approach the holiday season. Let us look past the hurts and tensions to the love that binds us together. Let us be a blessing for one another.

December 5

Repent, for the kingdom of heaven has come near. (Matthew 3:2)

These were the first words of John the Baptist as he proclaimed the coming of Jesus. In order for us to prepare the way for Jesus, we first must repent. *Repent* literally means "return." John was telling the people of Israel to come back to the way of life established by their Covenant with God. We too have a covenant, or an agreement, with God that was established at our baptism. Do you need to make changes in your life in order to return to it? How can you make the necessary changes?

God, I know that you love me. Help me to be true to that love and to my commitment to follow you. Help me repent, or return to you.

For more: Read more about the Covenant established between God and Israel. See Exodus 19:3–6, Exodus 24:3–8, and Jeremiah 31:31–34.

SAINT NICHOLAS (FOURTH CENTURY)

How beautiful upon the mountains are the feet of the messenger who announces peace, who brings good news, who announces salvation. (Isaiah 52:7)

Not much is known about Saint Nicholas except that he was a bishop in Asia Minor. Many legends have sprung up around this popular saint, and most of them have to do with his generosity and kindness, especially to those in need. In the United States, Saint Nicholas evolved into Santa Claus, who has become a symbol for the spirit of giving that we associate with the holiday season. Today is a good day to reflect on who really needs your help and generosity.

God of gladness, as I approach the birth of your Son, today's feast is a reminder to me of the joy that awaits us at Christmas. Help me to never lose sight of the true meaning of Christmas that Saint Nicholas points us to: we are called to give generously to those in need.

December 7

Prepare the way of the Lord! (Isaiah 40:3, Matthew 3:3)

Advent is a time of preparation for the arrival of the Savior. How can we prepare? A few ideas: set aside more time each day to pray; spend some time with someone who needs a friend; write to, call, or e-mail a lonely relative weekly; keep a daily journal; make peace with someone in your life. Is there something you can do in your daily life to prepare for the coming of the Savior?

Help me to prepare my heart for Jesus' coming, loving God.

For more: Read Isaiah, chapter 40, again.

MARY

A woman who fears the Lord is to be praised. Give her a share in the fruit of her hands, and let her works praise her in the city gates. (Proverbs 31:30–31)

Mary's unique role as the mother of Jesus calls for celebration. On this holy day, we celebrate Mary's conception. Like all humans, Jesus was born of a woman, Mary. Her consent to God's invitation attests to her great love of God and her willingness to do God's will. Her birthday is certainly something to be remembered.

Hail Mary, full of grace, the Lord is with you. Blessed are you among women, and blessed is the fruit of your womb, Jesus. Holy Mary, mother of God, pray for us sinners, now and at the hour of our death.

December 9

And now, you will conceive in your womb and bear a son, and you will name him Jesus. (Luke 1:31)

Mary was single and pregnant in a time when it was not only looked down on but it was against the law! Her nine-month preparation for Jesus' birth was filled with all the human challenges of pregnancy. She also had to deal with being pregnant before being officially married. One way to prepare your heart is to put yourself in Mary's shoes. If you were asked to do the impossible, knowing you would be ridiculed, or worse, how would you prepare your heart?

All things are possible with you, God. Help me to believe this and to prepare my heart to do the things you ask of me.

For more: Jonah was asked to do what he considered to be the impossible, as was Simon of Cyrene. Would you have done the same if you were in their shoes? Read the Book of Jonah and Luke 23:26.

My soul magnifies the Lord. (Luke 1:46)

How exactly does one magnify the Lord, especially with one's soul? To magnify means to make something bigger so that we can take a better look at it. A soul is the essence of a person. To magnify God means to make God bigger to other people. Does your life, your being, make God bigger to others? Think of one thing you can do today to magnify God.

God, I hope that my soul magnifies you. Help me to show your love to others.

For more: Read the entire Magnificat, Mary's prayer, found in Luke 1:46–55.

December 11

Like a bird that strays from its nest is one who strays from home. (Proverbs 27:8)

The image presented here of a bird that has strayed from the nest is a reminder to us that home is where we belong, or else we will become a stray. Reflect on all the good things about having a home and being at home.

Dear God, it is easy for us to get frustrated with our home and our family. When I think of straying, remind me of those who are truly homeless and are without the blessings of shelter and warmth, especially at this time of the year. Thank you for the gift of home.

OUR LADY OF GUADALUPE

Speak out for those who cannot speak, for the rights of all the destitute. Speak out, judge righteously, defend the rights of the poor and needy. (Proverbs 31:8–9)

In December 1531 Mary appeared to Juan Diego on a hillside near present-day Mexico City. She looked just like the native women of Mexico. To persuade a skeptical bishop that Mary had come to him, Juan Diego opened his cloak, and roses spilled out, a rarity in December. Much more significant was the miraculous image of Our Lady on his cloak. That image on cactus cloth has survived and is displayed at the Basilica of Our Lady of Guadalupe in Mexico City. This event resulted in the conversion of nine million native Mexicans to Christianity. Jesus, as Mary revealed, belongs to poor people, not just to the powerful.

God, on this day set aside to honor Our Lady of Guadalupe, we pray especially for the people of Mexico and Central America. May Mary and Jesus continue to inspire them and give them hope.

December 13

See, the home of God is among mortals. He will dwell with them as their God; they will be his peoples, and God himself will be with them. (Revelation 21:3)

Why don't you think about buying God (who dwells with and in us) a present? Obviously it will not be possible to give God something tangible, but you can give something tangible to someone in whom God dwells and who is in need. Can you find some money to buy a toy for a needy child or to donate to a family living in poverty? It might be the best present God ever gets.

Help me to find you in everyone, God, for you dwell among us.

For more: Read Genesis, chapter 18, in which Abraham takes care of God's messengers without even knowing it.

JOHN OF THE CROSS (1542–1591)

The true light, which enlightens everyone, was coming into the world. (John 1:9)

Today is the feast of John of the Cross, a fifteenth-century Spanish mystic, best known for his religious poetry. One of his most famous works refers to God as "The Living Flame of Love." About the birth of Jesus, he wrote: "The joy of God in men was seen. / Two things so alien to each other, / Or to the rule, had never been." Jesus shows that God does take joy in humanity. What does God see in you that would make God rejoice?

God, thank you for the gift of your flame of love. May I always feel it burning within me.

For more: John of the Cross was heavily influenced by the Song of Solomon, found in the Hebrew Scriptures. Take some time to read a chapter or two.

December 15

Remember then from what you have fallen; repent, and do the works you did at first. (Revelation 2:5)

If you ran into a good friend that you hadn't seen in a long time, would he or she still know you? Are you still the same person, or have you changed? Advent is the time to repent, or return. What are some good habits and some bad habits that you have developed? What can you do to grow in the good habits and to return "from what you have fallen"?

God of compassion, habits—especially bad habits—are hard to break. Give me strength and willpower that I may return to a better state.

For more: Read about the conversion of Saul in Acts of the Apostles, chapter 9.

He [Jesus] is the image of the invisible God. (Colossians 1:15)

We can never really wrap our mind around the concept of God. Augustine, the great theologian, says that if we have understood God, then what we have understood is not God. But we have been given the image of God in a concrete, human way in Jesus. Jesus is God in human form, in a form that we can see and understand.

God, thank you for giving yourself to the world that we may better know you.

For more: Jesus tells of his relationship to God in John 5:25–47.

December 17

Come, Lord Jesus! (Revelation 22:20)

Over and over during Advent, we pray, "Come, Lord Jesus!" but are we really ready to make that prayer? Inviting Jesus to come into our heart is like inviting company over for dinner: we need to be prepared for them. We need to know what we are going to serve, if we have enough food, if we have places for everyone to sit, and so on. Are you ready to invite Jesus into your heart? Have you made all your preparations? What preparations do you still need to make?

Jesus, I want to be truly ready when you come. Help me with my preparations so I can honestly say, "Come, Lord Jesus!"

For more: One way to prepare is to read the Christmas story again. Look at Matthew, chapters 1 and 2.

Yes, Lord, I believe that you are the Messiah, the Son of God, the one coming into the world. (John 11:27)

At a moment of profound grief over the death of her brother, Martha spoke these words to Jesus. She did not complain or become angry. Rather, she offered a moving profession of her belief in Jesus. What do we say to God in our darkest times? Do we really believe that Jesus is "the Messiah, the Son of God, the one coming into the world"? Try praying Martha's words over and over about something difficult in your life to see if these words give you a new perspective.

I believe that you sent your Son into the world for us, God. Help me to draw strength from your presence, even when all I feel is despair.

For more: Read the story of the raising of Lazarus (John 11:1–44).

December 19

You will know the truth, and the truth will make you free. (John 8:32)

Have you ever told a little lie, only to have it get a little bigger to protect the original lie? Pretty soon you have one huge, complex lie on your hands, and you can't remember who you told what to. Then when you finally tell the truth, a huge weight is lifted off your shoulders. Believing in Jesus is a little like that. In doing a little evil, we begin to tell a little lie to God. Before we know it, the lie is bigger than we are. But being true to our faith will keep us free and allow us to start each day with integrity and peace of mind.

I know the truth is not always easy. Help me to live your truth every day, O God.

For more: Read John 8:12–58, which talks about truth and freedom.

Darkness would not be dark to you; night would shine as the day. (Psalm 139:12)

We encounter a lot of hours of darkness during these December days. Many people are afraid of the dark. It is good to recall that to God, there is only light. God is the source of all light, and to be in God's presence is to be dazzled by brightness. How can we be light to others today?

God, during these long, dark winter nights, we are reminded of your light. Help me to be a bearer of light to illuminate the darkness in our world. You are the source of the light in my life.

WINTER SOLSTICE

Bless the Lord, winter cold and summer heat; sing praise to him and highly exalt him forever. (Daniel 3:67)

Today in the northern hemisphere marks the shortest day of the year and the beginning of winter. Christmas, the birth of the Light of the World, is only a few short days away. In the southern half of the world, just the opposite is happening: it is the beginning of summer and the longest day of the year. Everywhere in the world, our attention is drawn to this season of light and warmth, the advent of the birthday of Jesus.

God of all light, as the birthday of Christ approaches, may I pause a moment on this solstice and thank you for the gifts of light and warmth, and especially the gift of your Son, to enlighten my life.

Seek Yahweh—constantly seek God's face. (Psalm 105:4)

God is present everywhere and always, but we need to remind ourselves of that simple but awesome reality. Look for simple ways to seek God's presence today, especially in the ordinary, routine parts of your day.

God always with me, people always seem to be looking for something. Help me to be a seeker of your presence. Open my eyes and heart to your presence. Give me your strength, and help me be truly present to others, especially to those in need.

December 23

How beautiful upon the mountains are the feet of the messenger who announces peace, who brings good news. (Isaiah 52:7)

There is a lot of good news in the air! We are rapidly approaching the feast of Christ's birth. How can we be messengers of the Good News today? Better yet, how can we *be* the Good News today?

God, help us to be messengers of peace and good news. There is so much good news to announce. Fill us with the energy we need to be messengers, and bless us as we strive to bring the Good News to others.

The Lord himself will give you a sign. Look, the young woman is with child and shall bear a son, and shall name him Immanuel. (Isaiah 7:14)

Immanuel, meaning "God is with us," is an incredible sign of God's love for us. God chooses one of us, a young woman, to bear Immanuel into the world. Jesus is the embodiment of God's promise to be with us. Reflect on this amazing sign of God's love for you.

God, on this Christmas Eve, I eagerly await the celebration of the birth of your Son to Mary. He is Immanuel, God-with-us, and he has changed the course of history. May I strive to focus on the birth of Jesus during these next few days. Jesus is the real present of Christmas.

CHRISTMAS DAY

The people who walked in darkness have seen a great light; . . . for a child has been born for us, a son given to us; authority rests upon his shoulders. (Isaiah 9:2–6)

No one has affected the human race as dramatically and significantly as Jesus, whose birthday we celebrate today. He was born poor and lived a relatively short life, but he touched many people, and he continues to give meaning to the lives of millions of people. The third millennium marks two thousand years of Christian history. Jesus still gives light in the darkness.

Saving God, with faith and joy I celebrate the birthday of Jesus, Immanuel. Increase our understanding and our love of the riches you have revealed in him who is light forever and ever.

STEPHEN, DEACON AND MARTYR

While they were stoning Stephen, he prayed, "Lord Jesus, receive my spirit." Then he knelt down and cried out in a loud voice. "Lord, do not hold this sin against them." (Acts of the Apostles 7:59–60)

Stephen is the first Christian martyr. The word *martyr* means "witness." Stephen was the first of many to live and die giving witness to their undying faith in Jesus. It is the courage and willingness of those first persecuted Christians that inspired so many others to follow this new faith. Would you have the courage to die for your faith?

Loving God, people today are still being persecuted for their belief in you. Thank you for the witness of so many brave and noble people who gave their lives to profess their faith in you. Strengthen my courage so that I can live as you have called me to live.

For more: Read the full story of Stephen in Acts of the Apostles, chapters 6 and 7.

THE APOSTLE JOHN

We declare to you what was from the beginning, what we have heard, what we have seen with our eyes, what we have looked at and touched with our hands, concerning the word of life. . . . This is the message we have heard from him and proclaim to you, that God is light and in him there is no darkness at all. (1 John 1:1–5)

John, along with his brother James, the sons of Zebedee, were two of the original Twelve chosen by Jesus, and John is also the author of one of the Gospels and two letters in the Bible. In John's Gospel he refers to himself as "the disciple whom Jesus loved," and he is the one to whom the crucified Jesus entrusted the care of his mother.

Holy Light, today we remember John, who left us many beautiful writings about Christ and the necessity of love. Help me to be a person of light, and to love, knowing that you are love.

THE HOLY INNOCENTS

When Herod saw that he had been tricked by the wise men, he was infuriated, and he sent and killed all the children in and around Bethlehem who were two years old or under. (Matthew 2:16)

The slaughter of the innocents is a well-known part of the Christmas story. It is yet another example of the horrible lengths to which tyrants will go to eliminate anyone who threatens their power. How could a king be so intimidated by a newborn baby? How could any human being carry out such an order?

Creator of us all, today we remember all the innocents who have suffered and died at the hands of the powerful. We remember the countless victims of genocide, abortion, infanticide, and child abuse. Bless the children who are so dear to you, and send your angels to watch over them.

December 29

I am the vine, you are the branches. (John 15:5)

We are connected to God like branches to a tree trunk. We are dependent on the vine for water, food—life itself. We cannot live apart from God. And yet most of us try to. We would much rather make our own decisions than pray about them, go against the Ten Commandments in a tiny way rather than consider them. Do you need help from God to prop up your branch? Just ask.

I don't always want to acknowledge my connection to you, my God, and what that connection means for my life. Help me to be more aware of you in my life.

For more: Read all of John, chapter 15.

My Father is glorified by this, that you bear much fruit and become my disciples. (John 15:8)

Just as branches cannot exist without the vine, the vine cannot do what it is supposed to do without the branches, for a vine ultimately needs to bear fruit. As branches connected to the vine of God, we are to "bear much fruit," sharing our many gifts with the world and with all those around us. In bearing fruit, God is glorified. What "fruit" do you bear? Would people be able to look at your fruit and know instantly that it grows from God's vine?

I want to glorify you, God, by using my gifts and bearing your fruit.

For more: First Corinthians, chapter 12, talks about the same thing, using "gifts" instead of fruit. Check it out.

December 31

Put away your former way of life, your old self . . . and be renewed in the spirit of your minds, and clothe yourselves with the new self, created according to the likeness of God in true righteousness and holiness. (Ephesians 4:22–24)

Another new year is approaching, another chance of renewal for each of us. Have you made a New Year's resolution? Is there something you could do for your faith life that would help you to "be renewed in the spirit of your mind and clothe yourself with a new self"?

Living God, may I tackle this coming year, striving toward "righteousness and holiness."

For more: In your process of renewal, begin by reading Psalm 51.

INDEX OF THEMES